AMAZON FBA:

THE BLACKBOOK - EVERYTHING YOU NEED TO KNOW TO START YOUR AMAZON BUSINESS EMPIRE

JOHN FISHER

Everything You Need to Know to Start Your Amazon Business Empire

TABLE OF CONTENTS

INTRODUCTION

What's that calling you? Amazon, the king of online retail. You see a great opportunity here because Amazon is the biggest in the market, and likely will continue to dominate well into the future. There are so many who want to jump on this bandwagon and enjoy the benefits of selling on Amazon.

You're among these people, and you want to set up a business without investing too much capital. Yet, how will you survive and set yourself apart from the tens and thousands of others in your position? In this book, I will guide you through the process.

First of all, thank you for downloading *Amazon FBA Blackbook: Everything You Need to Know to Start Your Amazon Business Empire*. In this book will teach you how to start your own Amazon trading business quickly and with minimal capital. I will show you the power of Amazon, and how you can use it to your financial advantage.

Unlike those "Get Rich Quick" books you find on the Internet all the time (which are total gimmicks, by the way), this book contains actual strategies used by thousands of people. Yes, you will have to put in some efforts, however, the payoff will be worth it. Trust me. People have created million-dollar empires with these strategies, and so can you.

So let's get started.

CHAPTER ONE

AMAZON IS THE BEST PLACE TO SELL

Sellers have a lot of choices these days because so many online retail websites have popped up in the market. People can sell their products through so many platforms and make a quick buck by selling off their old (and sometimes, new) stuff. You can also start a serious business if that's what you want. Most of these e-commerce platforms don't care either way, so making a choice between popular ones can be difficult for the newbie.

If you're looking for serious business, though, Amazon is the best choice for you. There are so many things Amazon makes easy for you. Below are some convincing reasons that Amazon is the best place to start your e-retail business:

Great Pricing: Amazon gives its sellers the most competitive prices in the market. Amazon's average selling price ("ASP") for most items is higher than most other similar sites, especially for the items it sells through fulfillment by Amazon ("FBA"). Another great thing about Amazon is that its customers are looking for options and ease of shopping, and not necessarily for the lowest prices or unique products.

Simplicity: The interface Amazon provides to its sellers is known for its elegance and simplicity, similar to its customer platform. It's much more efficient and professionally competent when compared to those of other e-retail platforms. With Amazon, things are much easier for you because you don't have to work with multiple third party platforms like PayPal. Nine out of 10 times, you can even get rid of most of your duties, like listing the product, managing your fees, getting products shipped, and shooting high quality photos for your products. Amazon makes everything in the trade easily work for you.

Visibility: It's much harder for small sellers to get visibility for themselves and their products on most e-retail platforms. They start out as a tiny part of a huge system, and it's really difficult to get to the top. Amazon gives the little guy much better visibility than any other platform. This is because Amazon uses a rotating search algorithm, which keeps shuffling search results for customers from time to time, giving new (and small) sellers better exposure. If you can afford to, you can even buy-sponsored links, which will drive much more traffic toward your products and boost your sales. You'll make healthy sales if you have a solid product.

Listing Fee: Most people who have worked in this business before have a fair idea about the margins. They're really tight, aren't they? That's the main reason why every seller wants to minimize listing fees. Once again, Amazon comes to your aid, saving you money. On Amazon, you don't have to pay any listing fee at all for most items. Some special types still require a listing fee, but it's so minimal compared to other platforms that you'll gladly pay it. This helps you keep your inventory flexible because your upfront costs are minimized.

Easy Order Fulfillment: Most e-retail platforms don't care about your shipping needs and how you're going to be able to ship your products to the customers on time. Amazon is different, and it makes *your* headache its own! If you want, Amazon can take care of all your orders and fulfill them for you. You don't have to work hard to fulfill orders yourself or maintain links with fulfillment partners. Amazon takes care of it for you, making your job much easier and keeps the system running smoothly.

Overhead Costs: Overhead costs are inevitable in any business, and every seller wants to minimize them. Amazon emerges as a champion for the sellers here, too. It helps you cut down your overhead costs in so many ways. You don't have to spend for high-resolution photos of your products, and there's no listing fee or maintenance cost most of the times. You even save on communication time. These low overhead costs makes Amazon one of the cheapest platforms available today.

Growth Prospects: Amazon leads the e-retail industry and it will continue to do so for the foreseeable future because of its efficiency and love for innovation. The market is expanding and Amazon will continue to grab a big part of it, thereby maximizing your exposure. This is the place for you to grow your business.

Integration: If you're among those people who don't want to deal with the trouble of interacting with a payment provider like PayPal, a market research provider like TeraPeak, a fulfillment partner like ShipWire or Fulfillrite, and don't want to choose what tools and listing formats to use, Amazon is your best option. It makes everything streamlined and easy for you to access without you having to make a lot of hard choices. You can do away with learning how to navigate through many different services because you manage everything from a single interface. You have full integration with all sorts of services, and everything can be controlled from your Amazon account.

Stability: Amazon has one of the most stable and efficient interfaces. It functions smoothly and isn't prone to frequent changes, so you don't have to go through multiple learning curve. So many other platforms keep changing their interface and workflows just to seem dynamic, but that can pose a problem to sellers. Amazon is very stable, so you don't have to worry too much about the constantly changing demographics, marketplace rules, fees, and features.

CHAPTER TWO

THE IMPORTANCE OF PRIVATE LABELING

Private labeling is very popular at the moment, so you have most probably heard of it. Most online retailers use private labeling for their products these days. This gives the products a unique identity that showcases the seller's brand. Private labeling also helps to market the product better and it creates a reputation for your brand. But how does it all happen?

First, you buy the products from a supplier to sell them under your brand name. You don't actually manufacture them, which is the conventional way of doing business. You create a private brand and then put all the products you buy under that brand name so you can resell them. For this, you need to get custom logos printed on the items and their packages, and get the previous brand identities (if any) removed. This ensures that the customer will associate the product with *your* brand, not with that of the manufacturer. This strategy is extremely popular right now and most online sellers use it. You can find companies that will help you in creating your own brand identity. They'll advise you on extending, promoting, and positioning your brand in the market, so you can make the best of it. J&D Consortium is a one example of such a company.

Let me tell you how a private label brand on your products helps your business.

Easier to handle: Trading is easier than manufacturing, that's pretty obvious. There's a lot less trouble, so throw away any misconceptions you might have about private labeling. Some people believe that selling products you manufacture yourself is the only way to roll and that private label products don't sell. Let me tell you that nothing is further from the truth. As long as you have a good quality product that you're selling at a fair price, nobody cares who manufactured it. Avoiding huge costs and selling under a private label is a wise decision.

Modification: With private labeling rights, you can make some modifications to the products according to your needs and wishes. This means you can make your products unique without having to come up with groundbreaking product ideas. Take products that are already in the market and make small changes to them to give them a personality. Private labeling is different from reselling, as reselling rights don't allow you to make any modifications, which isn't the case with private labeling rights. So come up with new ideas and incorporate them into your product design. It's your product, do what you want!

Customer Satisfaction: Private labeling makes things easier for you by removing steps in your business journey. Initially, when you do private labeling, you won't need to spend time on product conceptualization, which is pretty difficult. By the way, even if you come up with a good product concept, someone will probably do it better than you, and you'll have to start over again. There are many giants in almost every industry niche, so it's futile to try and beat them at their own game. Instead, just buy the products and give them your personal brand. That allows you to concentrate on other important things like customer satisfaction. Your maximum attention will go to your customers because you don't have to worry about stuff like personnel management, product planning, efficiency control, and other big tasks.

Riding the Bandwagon: When you introduce a new product in the market, it's always risky. New ideas tend to be like that by nature. They'll either be super flops or super hits most of the times, and one can never be sure. A high margin of error makes things expensive and difficult for the manufacturer if the product fails. It's not the road for everyone. Private labeling, however, is much easier. You don't have to worry about losing money since you can pick an already popular product and sell it under your private label brand to benefit from its popularity. You'll get a customer base with minimal effort, and without having to spend much money on promotion.

HOW TO CHOOSE THE BEST PRIVATE LABEL PRODUCTS FOR AMAZON FBA

One of the most popular practices for selling on Amazon FBA is private label products, but the problem that most people struggle with is working out which products to sell; that is, what the best ones are to build their own brand around. There are people who choose the complicated route, choosing items that need a lot of modification and cost a fortune to produce, and there are those who choose the easier route.

The first question to ask yourself is why you are choosing private labelling. Most people who choose to use Amazon to create their brand are fed up with trying to find decent goods on eBay that they can flip on Amazon for a profit, or vice versa. Reselling is not a good game to get into – it might bring you a little extra cash but it will never be a stable income and there is a lot of work involved.

Private label products give you the best chance at a consistent and relatively passive income, while keeping labor, time expended, and overhead costs to a minimum. Most people can see the real benefits to building their brand around private label products without the need to keep on looking for new ones to keep the money rolling in. However, there is one huge hurdle that stands in their way of true success – unnecessary complication.

KEEP IT SIMPLE

It is easy to see the benefits of brand building; but, the more complex a product you choose, the more work has to be put into it in order to have a much better chance of generating revenue. Ok, that may be true; after all, the iPhone is far more valuable than a pack of plastic food containers, but building a new iPhone does not mean that people are going to buy it. The most success and money you make will come from simple items.

When it comes down to the crunch, the best private label products to build your brand around are simple and, if you follow these rules, you will find it works. Ask yourself these questions before you put your money down on a particular product:

- **Is it evergreen?** Will your customer keep on coming back to it, time and time again? Think about things like shampoo or conditioner – items that people will buy over and again.

- **Is your product something that people are looking for?** Imagine that you just blew a couple of thousand dollars on a product, branded it and then found that nobody is actually looking for that particular product. Not just your actual brand, but the product type itself. How would you feel? Gutted? Stupid? Do your homework first. There is an easy way to find out what people are looking for on Amazon before you lay out your life savings and that is to run a keyword search on Amazon. You can do this by typing in specific keywords to the search bar on Amazon and see what the results are so you can use one of the many automatic tools to search for you. Some of these tools will tell you what has been searched for on specific listings and others will identify market gaps that you can think about jumping into.

- **Does your product have tons of competition?** If you choose a product that is extremely common on Amazon, you might struggle to get your foot in the door. However, there are quite a few products that are lacking in competition and these are the ones that you should look at. Even if the item does have competition, consider if you can come up with something the competition can't like providing multiples.

- **How easy and cheap is the product to produce?** You do not need to sell expensive items that cost a fortune to make and involve a lot of modification. It's better to sell 15 units of plastic container packs a day at $20 each than it is to sell a phone that has an extremely low profit margin once in a while.

- **Are there any proven sales data against this product?** One step that many people skip over is testing their Amazon listing with retail store products, before choosing to place a bulk order. This is an important step and one that will show whether your product will sell before you start the expensive step of sourcing your product from a manufacturer.

There is nothing too scientific or difficult about this. The very best products to sell under private label are simple ones: items that will stand the test of time, products that people come back to time and time again.

5 MORE RULES FOR PRIVATE LABEL SELLING ON AMAZON FBA

By now you should already know how to get going with private label selling on Amazon FBA. However, there are still those that think it is going to be a simple job and that they can make money instantly. The following are the five most important rules to private label selling on Amazon:

You Need Capital

This is the most important rule – you cannot make money with private label selling unless you have the capital to lay out in the initial stage. You can't buy your stock, build your brand, and design your packaging without having a lot of capital to start off with. Creating your very own private label is NOT the same as finding a resell product to flip on Amazon. You need the money to buy your product in bulk and to pay for any modifications. Initially, your suppliers are not going to give you the best deal on your chosen product and they certainly won't build any prototypes for you unless you are going to purchase vast quantities – that means money, and possibly a lot of it. If you don't have it or are not prepared to pay out, go away and find another avenue because you will be wasting your time.

You Are Not Going to Get Any Quick Wins

There is a big difference between the person who resells on Amazon and those who come up with their own products and brands. Those who do the latter are building up an asset, something that will bring the money in for the foreseeable future, whereas a reseller is simply making immediate money and will need to go off and find another product to sell afterwards.

There is a world of difference between these two types of personality. Everyone wants to make money but the person who builds an asset knows that, even if their product only draws in an extra couple of hundred dollars a month, it is far superior and lasts a lot longer than the person who flips an expensive item. Why is this?

Assets are always the better option than just having the know-how to flip a single product. Assets have a more sustainable value; they will last through time. It is far better to have 10 assets worth $500 that make you $5000 per month and every month than to resell products that you flip once and they're gone.

Know Who Your Customers Are and Keep Your Risks Low

One of the most profitable ways to have success with a private label product is to know exactly who your customers are and to understand them. And the best way to understand your customers is to use Amazon Sponsored Ads.

The stupidest thing to do would be to pick a product, talk to your supplier, buy a whole load, and stick it on Amazon expecting to make a ton of money. It can work but success is very rare with that kind of haphazard operation. You need to keep your risks low when you are creating your private label product. Use Amazon Sponsored Ads to test out your product to ensure that this is something people really want and will dig into their wallets for. You need to shift your mindset for this but learn how to use these sponsored ads to your advantage before you pay out for something you can't shift.

You Are Not an Amazon Reseller So Stop Thinking Like One

Lots of people get into trouble by thinking like an Amazon reseller and not like a private label seller. To be successful and to run a real business you have to spend time building your brand and your assets. The assets you build are going to generate money with very little involvement from you. A reseller has to restart every week or month, looking for that next big product to flip, processing their shipments and everything else that goes with it. A private label seller who has done their homework can build something that is much bigger than they are, something that lasts for the long term.

Don't Forget to Build on the Success of Your Work

Last, and most important, build on your success. The money that you earn from your product needs to go into creating another one and sustaining it. It is so tempting to take your earnings and spend it but, as with anything, the more you put back in, the more you will get out.

To be successful at selling private label products, you have to keep in mind that they are not easy to create and it will be a very rare person who hits the home run on the first try. Don't despair; do your homework and test out your products before you buy them and start small. Build your business as you go and, if you do it right, you will eventually have a stable of assets that consistently generate revenue with little input from you.

These reasons should be more than good enough to convince you. As an online retailer, you should definitely consider private labeling, as it will take your business to the next level much faster.

Now, let's discuss how you can start your business with Amazon.

CHAPTER THREE

SETTING UP A SELLER ACCOUNT

Amazon gives you a big opportunity to make money online. You can earn some extra income from it, or you can even quit your job and set up a full-time business on Amazon if you want to. Amazon gives you a lot of freedom and you can take out more than what you put into it.

Let me list some of the benefits of selling on Amazon:

- Flexible work schedule and freedom of work

- Financial security

- Good returns on your investments

- More free time to enjoy the things you love doing

- Experience to carry out bigger projects in future

It's so easy that pretty much anyone can learn to do it, and that's the best thing about it. You have control over how profitable your business will be. Your efficacy in applying the strategies mentioned will decide how successful you are. Gradually, you will also learn the ins and outs of the trade, and this will boost your income further. All of that, however, comes later. Right now, we must start with some baby steps. Creating an Amazon Seller Central account is your first step to starting your business.

The process is pretty straightforward. Amazon has given helpful tips to get you through it easily, and you don't need to follow anything else. I'll simplify the process for you here:

1) Open the following URL in your web browser" sellercentral.amazon.com.

2) There will be a login page. When you click on the "Register Now" button on the login panel, it will take you to a different page.

3) The first thing you have to do here is to choose whether you will be selling as an "Individual" or as a "Professional." Let's take a look at the differences between these two.

a) An Individual seller can only sell a maximum of 40 items in a month. A Professional seller, on the other hand, can sell any number of items in a month. There are no restrictions.

b) An Individual seller is charged a commission of 99 cents on each item that he sells. There's no monthly fee in this case. A Professional seller pays a monthly fee of $39.99. In either case, you may have to pay some additional fees at times, like referral fees and variable closing fees.

c) Professional sellers can sell items in all categories available on Amazon. Individual sellers can't do that. They're allowed to sell in only limited number of categories. So it's advisable that you go with the "Professional" plan for your business.

4) Once you choose a plan, you will have to read a seller agreement and sign it.

5) Print out this agreement before you go any further. This will help you iron out any issues in the future. Once you've read it, agree to the terms and conditions, and then proceed further.

6) In the next window, you will need to fill in some important information, such as your credit card details, billing address, seller name, and your business address.

7) After this, you will need to verify your identity. A PIN will be given to you through a text or a phone-call on a number that you provide them. This is a standard procedure that many sites follow.

8) A Professional seller also has to provide the necessary tax information to Amazon in order to proceed.

9) Once you've provided your tax information, the registration procedure will be complete and you'll be taken to the home page of your Seller Central account. From here, you can manage all activities in your account.

There are several tabs in the top navigation bar of your home page. Let me give you a walk-through of these tabs.

- Inventory: You can add new products and manage existing ones from here.

- Reports: This tab lets you view all your payment reports and tax info.

- Orders: Check all the received orders and handle all the returns from here.

- Performance: All the feedback you receive from customers is shown here, along with any claims they made and other performance-related information.

- Settings: In this tab, you can change any of your account information.

SETTING UP YOUR SELLER PROFILE

When your account has been activated, you will need to complete your public profile. This is what prospective customers will look at, so consider it as the Amazon version of your Facebook or Twitter profile. Your customers will get to know who you are, what your business is all about, and what shipping options you offer. They will see your returns policy, feedback from other customers, and much more.

The main parts of your profile that you should concentrate on are:

- *About Seller*

This section is where you get to introduce yourself and your business to your customers. You need to tell people exactly who you are, how your business started, and what inspired it. Explain your business philosophy, what you want to achieve and offer to your customers, and tell them anything else that is relevant. You are trying to create a connection to your customers and you need to be as transparent as possible. This will help to build up trust and your customers will be more likely to choose you over your competition.

- *Your Logo*

Prospective customers will be able to see your logo in a number of places, including the Offer Listing page, on your storefront, and on your "At a Glance" page. Keep your logo to 120 x 30 pixels and do not include any URLs or references to your website in it.

- *Your Return and Refunds Policies*

Give your customers full instructions on how they can return items for a refund or a replacement. Let them know the address they need to send returns to and tell them approximately how long it will take you to process a refund or send out a replacement product. When you are setting up your policies, do bear in mind that Amazon has a requirement that all sellers allow customers to return goods for a minimum period of 30 days after the sale.

With this information in hand, you can create your Amazon Seller Central account, start listing your products and making money!

CHAPTER FOUR

PICKING A GREAT PRODUCT

This is possibly the most important step in the whole process. It will all be for naught if you fail to choose a winning product. Why is it so important? Simply because the only way for your business to succeed is for you to pick a product that sells well. For a product to sell more units, it has to be marketable. Without a great product, you can't make your business work.

So what makes a product "great"? Let's take a look at some important factors.

GOOD SALES VOLUME

This is an elementary rule for choosing a good product. You want to sell this product, so you need to make sure it will sell well. If you pick a niche product that only sells a couple of units every month, you won't make much profit at all. There is a lot of competition, so you must pick a product that is selling big. But it's also important that there are no big players already selling that product. These sellers tend to dominate the markets they're selling in, taking up most of the market share by selling at low margins. This is because they enjoy the economies of large scale that small sellers can't.

ATTRACTIVE PRICING

If you're familiar with a behavioral concept called **impulsive buying**, you know how important it is to put the right price on your product. You need to pick a product that falls into the right price bracket. It should be priced high enough that people don't think of it as a useless trinket, but inexpensive enough that people feel the urge to buy it as soon as they see the price. This is what we call impulsive buying. When the customer thinks the price isn't too high, she doesn't consider making comparisons with similar products, which gives you a competitive advantage.

Since you have to pay some fees to Amazon, you can't pick a product that is very cheap, because you won't profit from it. The best price range is between $20 and $100. If you want to refine it even further, pick a product below $50.

NICHE PRODUCT

Extremely generic products won't sell, at least not for your business. So if you were thinking of going with clothes or soap bars, drop the idea. Your products need to be a bit unique, so they can serve a particular niche. Markets of generic products are highly saturated already, and they have big players dominating the field, so you don't want to go there. Instead, you need to target a specific group of customers, a group that isn't too big or too small, but just the right size to give you profitable returns. Sell a product that people can't easily find in supermarkets or malls in every city, something that isn't mainstream.

NON-SEASONAL PRODUCT

You want to make year-round sales? Simple--don't pick a seasonal product. You'll be amazed at how many people don't consider this before choosing the right product for their business. If you wish to sell throughout the year, pick a product that is not seasonal in nature. Otherwise, your sales will drop hard when people don't need your product, and it will hurt your business. If you must sell a seasonal product, pick a few other products to sell, too, and make sure some of them are non-seasonal. This way, you can keep selling throughout the year.

NECESSARY COMPETITION

Not all competition is bad competition; realize this before you start selling. A small seller like you cannot afford to spend much on advertising your product, so it's good to have some competition in your market. It's healthy for your business, even advantageous. Being the only player in the market won't benefit you, since you won't be able to create awareness for your product in the market.

So pick a product that has a healthy level of competition. This will ensure that you can reap the benefits of your competitors' advertising. At the same time, be wary of oversaturated markets. Too much competition will kill your business, as discussed earlier.

GOOD SUPPLIER

Good suppliers are indispensable to a business. You can trust a good supplier to deliver the right goods on time. This will ensure that you can fulfill orders on time and will help to build and maintain your reputation. On the other hand, a bad supplier will be unreliable, which can hurt your business if he doesn't deliver on time.

It's ideal to have a reputed supplier for your chosen product(s), and best to have multiple suppliers. That way you can make sure your sales aren't hampered even if one seller is facing some issue.

MOBILITY

The mobility of your product is also an important factor. You should pick a product that is easy to ship because Amazon enforces strict standards about packaging and shipping. You can run into problems if your product is too fragile, bulky, or easily damaged. Drop tests are used to check the packaging of most products. This determines whether they can be shipped safely.

PROFITABILITY

This is the most obvious one. What's the point of selling a product if you can't profit from it, right? You're in the business to make a profit and that's impossible without a profitable product. So make sure the product you choose to sell allows you decent profit margins, even after paying the Amazon fees.

Now that we've taken a look at some of the most important factors in determining what product(s) to sell, you must be wondering how to find the right product. Let's give you a head start.

The easiest way to start is by looking at the Amazon best sellers page. This page is updated on an hourly basis, and here you can find the best-selling items on the website. Amazon uses complex algorithms to give you highly accurate and reliable results. Visit www.amazon.com/gp/bestsellers and browse for a while. Eventually, you will find a product you can easily brand and start selling.

If this is not enough, you can check other venues, too. The Movers & Shakers section and the Hot New Releases section will tell you about products that are selling well at the moment. Amazon also has wish lists, so you can check in the Most Wished for section to get an idea. You can also get ideas from the Gift Ideas section. Make a small list of products, and then check each one against the parameters we discussed earlier. This will help you pick the best product to sell.

There are other places to look for potential products if you're still not satisfied. Check eBay, Google shopping, and other popular e-commerce websites.

Here's a small checklist of things you should do when deciding on a product:

- Check the demand for the product by going through the bestsellers list or using the Google Keyword tool

- Make sure the product isn't seasonal in nature

- Check that the product is appropriately priced to encourage impulsive buying

- Check that there are no big players in the market already selling that product

- Make sure you can easily ship the product

- See to it that there are good suppliers available for the product

VIABILITY CHECKLIST

Now, there are Amazon sellers who seem to be able to judge the market but get nothing else right and still make money. There are also those sellers who get the market terribly wrong but do everything else right and don't make a lot of money. That goes to show that the market you are targeting is important, but so is getting everything else right. Together with everything else in this chapter, I am giving you another way to make sure that you get the right product and the right market; a way of scoring your choices to see if you should go ahead or call it quits before you lay out any money or time.

The following checklist is easy to use and will help you to determine if your product is viable and if your market is viable. The system will tell you whether you should carry on with your private label venture or keep on searching. Each line has a score beside it –give yourself that score if you can answer yes or a zero if the answer is no. At the end, we will tally up the points and see where you are.

MARKET VIABILITY

Does a National Brand Name Dominate in the Market? If Not, Score 5

If your product is in competition with a national brand then, in all honesty, you may as well give up. Let's say you choose to go with cameras; the likes of Nikon and Canon would just push you into insignificance. Think about going with items such as kitchen accessories or any other kind of accessory where there no national brand name rules the market.

Is the Average Sales Price Somewhere Between $15 and $60? Score 5

One vital point to keep in mind is that you need some margin to pay for your marketing. If you sell something that is worth $50, you will have to do the same amount of work as you would if you were selling items that cost no more than $7 to $10. Unless you are running a big name department store, you will find it very hard to win the low profit/high volume game.

Is the Sales Rank for the Top Three Items Below 10,000? Score 4

When you choose a product, you must make sure that it will sell in sufficient volume to meet the goals you set for income. Don't create a product for which is there is little to no demand; it will be a waste of your time and money. Much will depend on the category that you choose and on the time of year, but take the following as a guide. Products in the range of 8000 and 10,000 are selling between 4 and 6 products per day; those in the 5000 to 8000 range will sell between 6 and 10, those that rank between 200 and 5000, around 10 to 20 items per day, and those that ran below 2000 are selling more per day than you can possibly count.

Do the Top Three Products Have 400 or Fewer Reviews – Score 4

Reviews are extremely important in getting a ranking for your product and convincing potential customers that they should buy from you and not from a competitor. While it is possible to get more than 400 reviews, it will take you a great deal of time, effort and, perhaps most important, money. If many products have fewer than 400 reviews, you have a viable chance to get in there and overtake them, using your excellent marketing skills.

Are There Any Page One Products with 100 or Fewer Reviews? Score 5

Money can be made with products that fall outside of the top three positions on page one. It could be that position number 6 or 7 can still earn you a potential $1,000 or more dollars every single month and there aren't too many people who would turn their noses up at that. When a reasonable number of products have 100 or fewer reviews, you have a good chance of getting on page one.

Are There Multiple Keywords for the Market? Score 5

Is your market likely to search for your product using a number of different keywords? The more keywords you have, the better your chance of making more sales. For example, if you are selling cutting boards, some people will use the search phrase "chopping boards". By using good marketing skills, you can get a good ranking for several different keywords, raising your sales and your profile significantly.

Are all Pay-Per-Click Ads in Use? Score 1

Take a look at your competitors – are they on the bottom or the side page PPC ad for long periods? If they are, it means that they are making good money from them and that is another market avenue to explore.

Is There a Product Video on Page One of the Google Search Results for the Top Keyword? Score 3

If there isn't, then get busy making a video. Create your own YouTube channel, if you don't already have one, and make some videos of your product. You could find yourself ranked on the Google search results and adding links to your videos will send people directly to your product page on Amazon.

Do the Top Three Keywords Have More Than 100,000 Combined Searches? Score 5

You can use a tool like Merchant Word to find this out. Do use it because this is a good way of making sure that there are sufficient searches to make your product viable.

Do the Top Listings Contain Knowledgeable Sellers? Score 4

This might sound somewhat counter-intuitive, but if other people are making some money in the market, you can come up with a product that is better, take better photos of those products, write better copy, and overtake them in the listings. This is also a validation test to show that there are sales for that particular product.

Can You Add Any Value to Your Product? Score 4

Always look at the negative reviews on your competitors' pages and see exactly what the customers are complaining about. Use the issues they raise to make your product better. For example, can you add an accessory to your product or bundle two items together or offer good discounts for buying in bulk? Make it something that a prospective customer will see as good value – do not forget that everyone likes to think they are getting something for free or cheaper than anyone else is.

Are the Products That Are in the Market Durable? Score 5

If the products are breakable or not designed to last very long, such as items made of glass, they tend to break when they are being shipped. Instead of blaming the shipping company, the customer will always lay the blame at your feet and give you bad reviews. It isn't your fault but, while this continues to happen, your sales will never rise.

Is the Product Easy to Use Without a Complicated Instruction Manual? Score 3

If a buyer doesn't understand how to use your product, it will always be your fault. And, as a punishment, they will give you a bad review. If they don't understand something, it will be your fault; if they don't use it properly, your fault. Go back to that cutting board we talked about earlier – a simple product that needs no explanation and no user manual. Compare that to an electronic product that might need assembling first and you can see where the problems lie.

Does the Product Lead to More Orders or Reorders? Score 5

Can you resell your product to the same customers over and over? Will they keep on coming back for more? That is the easiest way to grow your business every month.

Can the Product Be Given as a Gift? Score 3

The biggest market these days is gift purchasing. If you can get your packaging to look like it is for a gift item, and the product itself is giftable, sales will rise quite significantly. You could find people ordering for themselves and then reordering as gifts for others.

Is the Product Something that Cannot Easily Be Purchased Elsewhere? Score 2

Commodity items like that ordinary cutting board can be bought anywhere, especially in big chain stores, and they are things that most people will buy from their local stores. If you were to make that cutting board into something special, with features that customers can't get elsewhere, they will come to you to make their purchase.

PRODUCT VIABILITY

Does the Product Weigh One Pound or Less? Score 4

The smaller a product is, the lighter it will be, usually. The lighter a product is, the less it costs to ship from your supplier and the lower your Amazon fees will be as well.

Is the Product Small? Score 4

Imagine an item that is about 8 inches by 8 inches by 8 inches; holding your hands together will usually give you an idea of how big this is. Now think about your product; is it bigger than that or smaller? If it is smaller than that, you can probably get yourself into the lowest fee bracket on Amazon, which means more money in your pocket.

Can the Product Be More Outstanding with Better Packaging? Score 5

Packaging is a huge part of this business. Good packaging encourages more sales and a higher price. Make your packaging attractive and suitable for the product.

Can You Buy Your Product with Shipping for 20% or Less of the Resale Price? Score 5

Amazon fees add up – their commission is 15% of your sales price; handling fees and packing fees start at $2.50. If your product has a sales price of $15, you would lose $2.25 in commission and about $2.50 for Amazon fees, leaving you $10.25 per item. Take off 20% for the cot price of the item and shipping and that leaves you a profit of $7.25 per item, equating to 47%. That is not bad for working from home in your PJs! If your shipping and costs come in at more than 20%, your profit will drop considerably.

Can You Make a First Purchase of 500 Units or Less? Score 4

You do not want to be laying out every penny you have on your initial order, but you do need enough products in stock to cover promotions and sales until you get enough money together to order more. Ordering too much will kill your profit stone dead.

Is your Product a Good Private Label Product for Amazon?

Add up the points you scored and use the following to determine if you should go ahead or call it a day:

- 0 - 40 points – Walk away now, don't look back.

- 40 – 50 points – You probably shouldn't do this, it will end up costing you.

- 50 to 65 points – You are looking pretty good here, it's well worth a shot.

- More than 65 – What are you waiting for? Get going, now!

This checklist is designed to give you an idea of whether you have the market and the product to make a serious go of Amazon FBA private label selling.

CHAPTER FIVE

FINDING THE RIGHT SUPPLIERS

Once you have one or more products that fit your criteria, you need to start looking for good suppliers for these products. This chapter will focus on how you can find the right supplier for your products quickly and efficiently.

The easiest way to do this is to look on www.alibaba.com. Alibaba is a website for traders. This site has a great number of manufacturers and suppliers of all sorts of products. You'll find sellers from pretty much everywhere in the world who trade in a wide variety of goods. Traders can contact them through the website and import products. You can still use trade magazines to find suppliers and manufacturers, as we used to do before the Internet, but Alibaba is definitely the easiest way to do this. It also gives you a lot of choice among sellers.

When you have decided which product(s) you want to sell, you can go and find them on Alibaba. There are plenty of suppliers for each product. It's not rare to find hundreds or even thousands of suppliers for a product, which makes choosing one supplier very difficult. Oh, the paradox of choice. I'll tell you something though – not all of them are relevant to you. So you can skip the irrelevant ones and narrow down your search by using the appropriate search filters.

Let's get you up to speed on some basics. Suppliers with a good reputation on the website are given the "Gold Supplier" tag. You can check under the supplier details how long a supplier has held that status. Then there are suppliers who are verified by Alibaba or a third party. Their factory or store has been visited by authorized personnel and they are listed under the "Onsite Check" filter. If a supplier has been inspected by a third party inspection company, they will be shown under the "Assessed Supplier" filter. If you wish to see the inspection report, that's available for you, too. An "Escrow" feature is available to ensure safe online payments, which makes sure payment is withheld to the supplier until safe delivery of goods has been made.

Using these filters will narrow down your search results considerably. Even so, you'll have a lot of options to look at. Now you should check the pricing and minimum units selling policy of each seller. In most cases, you'll find that these numbers are negotiable, so contact a few sellers before you settle on one.

Start with six suppliers. Contact each of them and let them know your requirements. Before you start negotiating the price and minimum order size with them, try to get a sample product. Your aim is to minimize price per unit without having to buy large quantities at once.

Discuss private labeling with them and let them know how you wish to brand the products. This is important because you want to create a brand identity for yourself in the market. Always ask the supplier beforehand whether they are willing to brand the products with your private label.

Avoid sellers who don't respond to your emails and messages in a timely manner. You don't want to deal with shoddy customer service.

Here are some tips to help you through the process:

1) Understand that finding the right supplier takes some time. There will be a fair amount of hit and miss before you settle on a supplier, so don't waste time looking for the perfect match. Try to get samples quickly from a few good suppliers instead.

2) You will probably settle on one supplier in the future, but you have to start with multiple suppliers in the beginning.

3) Alibaba has a sister site: www.aliexpress.com. Here, you can place smaller orders and get samples to test.

4) Treat your samples as your investment. Instead of selling them on Amazon, put them through some rough tests to see how durable they are. You don't want unsatisfied customers, so it's important that you do this.

5) Placing a big first order isn't necessary. There are a lot of factors that determine the size of your initial order: your capital; product demand; price per unit; and other things. Start by ordering a few units from Aliexpress if you believe that it is necessary.

6) Even if you have substantial capital to begin with, don't place a big order when you start. You first need to do some test marketing to help you ascertain the profitability and demand of the product you're selling. Once you have gauged all that, you can start placing larger orders. This also gives you opportunity to switch suppliers without suffering loss, in case you are dissatisfied with one supplier.

7) Your relationship with your supplier(s) will become stronger as your sales increase and become more consistent. You will soon be able to get better quotes from

them, and some might even offer additional services such as customer service and shipping. This will help you automate much of your business.

SHIPMENT METHODS

You may not realize this right now, but choosing the right shipping method is very important to the success of your business. It's an important decision that will decide how your business operates. Your initial investment has a big role to play in this decision, along with the availability of workforce. Most sellers start with private shipping or FBA. Whatever you start with, though, you should aim to get your products drop shipped once your business picks up pace.

Private Shipping

Many people start with this by turning their garage into a temporary warehouse. If you don't have much capital in the beginning, you can start with private shipping, too. Store your products in your garage when your supplier sends them to you, and ship them to your customers whenever you get an order. When you are just starting out, you don't have many orders, so this approach works well.

It helps you add a personal touch to all your orders. You can add a customized note when packaging your product, thanking the customer for the purchase and telling them a bit more about your brand information. You can add your web address on the note. If your product is good and your packaging efficient, it leaves a good impact on the customer and helps you connect with them emotionally.

For this method to work, you need to be good at time management, because shipping products on time is of paramount importance. Everything will be handled by you personally, which can be either really motivating or really stressful. You need to be able to handle it all well.

Make sure you switch to better methods of shipping once your business has picked up pace.

Fulfillment by Amazon

FBA becomes an efficient way to complete orders once you've started to sell well. It helps you automate part of your business and let Amazon take care of it for you. Amazon charges a small fee for handling the whole shipping process for you. All you have to do is ship your products to an Amazon warehouse. You can even ask your supplier to ship directly to an Amazon warehouse, which further cuts your costs. This saves you both time and money.

We'll learn more about FBA in an upcoming chapter.

Drop Shipping

Drop shipping is a widely popular method of shipping products. It's used by many online retailers all over the world. Products are sent by the suppliers directly to the customers. The trader, i.e. you, has no part in it, so you don't have to worry about packaging and shipping the product yourself. If you are a regular customer and bring decent business to a supplier you work with, he will agree to drop ship the items for you. What's more, the supplier might even offer to handle all customer service for you, which automates your business a great deal.

When you build such a relationship with a supplier, your business will evolve to another level of automation. You will only have to manage the front-end of the business, and you can pay attention to things like marketing and brand promotion. The supplier will take care of the back-end for you.

PRIVATE LABELING

For most suppliers, adding a private label to the products they sell to you isn't anything out of the ordinary. They'll easily agree to do it for you. In fact, many of them even have ready-made templates for your designs and logos to place the products. Once you have a logo designed for your brand, you can choose a template and have your logo printed on the product packages. It's a really easy way to create an identity for your brand.

First, you need to come up with a nice, creative name for your brand, so that the customers can associate your product with it. It's also something to remember your product by. Once you've done that, you should get your logo designed. You can create your own logos at websites like www.logoyes.com, or hire a designer to do it for you. A couple of websites where you can look for freelance designers are upwork.com and www.fiverr.com. There are others, too. You can find freelancers who will do this for you at a fairly reasonable price.

The next step is to pick a box design, if needed, and get a UPC code for your product. Ideally, you should also register your trademark with the appropriate authority so it can't be copied.

Once you're done with all this, contact your supplier and ask them to print your private label on all your products.

THE IMPORTANCE OF SAMPLES

This is an important step. You probably wonder why it is so important. After all, you know what your product looks like; you know how it works so why do you need a sample of it?

First, you may be thinking about buying a product that needs a little modification to make it truly original for you. In that case, you need to see how that sample looks, how it works (if, indeed, it works), and if it is what you are looking for.

You should try to order at least three samples of your product if you can, especially if you are making changes. If you are selling in different colors, ask for a sample in each color so you can see how they look. You want to see how the samples are packaged into your choice of box, to make sure it is right for the product. If you order just one sample and it was tossed into the box without any padding, you won't know if this is a one-off or the way they normally package the goods. Ordering a number of samples will answer that question.

Costing

If you are customizing your product, the price will obviously rise and so will the cost of the samples. Let's say it cost you $100 for each sample (these are just figures plucked out of the air so don't panic!), you ordered three and paid for shipping. The samples would cost you $300 and shipping, for arguments sake, $150 (these are big items – smaller ones cost less, obviously). That is a total of $450 to create and ship your three samples. Now, that might sound like a lot of money just for samples, but here is why it is important.

First, you get to see the quality of the product. If you were to just buy thousands of units without testing them, you could find that you are trying to sell a piece of poorly made rubbish. Paying for the samples allows you to see what they are like first. Poor products will earn you nothing more than a bunch of requests for refunds and a bad reputation. Second, you can see each variation of the product to determine which ones work best and which you might drop. Third, you can test the product yourself, which is worth all the money you spend. At least you will know that the product works and is of quality.

HOW TO USE YOUR SAMPLES

When you order these samples, you should first do check out the quality, but there are a few other things that you can do to get your money's worth. Here are the best ways to make use of your samples:

1. **Use Them for The Photos for Your Amazon Listing**

When your supplier sends you pictures of your product, they are probably not of the best quality and certainly not a very good representation of what you are selling. People like to see good clear pictures of a product they are interested in and poor quality image are a big turn-off.

Many customers determine, on the basis of the images, whether they want to buy the product or not, so you need to have the best quality images you can. Using the samples, you can photograph each variation and each color and you can photograph the product from different angles as well. Use a decent quality camera or smartphone to take your photos with and get the best that you can without hiring a professional photographer. If you do find that you have to use a professional, you can send one of your samples away and still have a couple left.

2. **Make Sure That the Packaging Looks Right**

Your suppliers will send you pictures of the packaging, but what you see in the picture and what the packaging actually looks like are two different things. In some cases, you may not even now what the packaging is going to look like. The packaging I am talking about here is the material that is packed with the product in the shipping box.

Let's say that you have ordered a case for the iPad. The case will arrive inside packaging that is inside the shipping box. A box inside a box, if you like. You need to be aware that you can put your own brand and design logo on this packaging to help build brand awareness; it doesn't have to be plain. Use your samples to work out what you want and how you want them packaged and speak to the supplier about making any changes that you want. Your packaging is the first thing that people see; if it isn't right, they won't have much confidence in the actual product. You can also use that packaging to advertise your own website and generate more traffic and more sales.

3. **Use Them to Get Feedback**

This is one of the very best things you can do with your samples. Show them to your family and friends and ask for their honest feedback. As a product owner you will have a certain amount of bias and it is good to get other people's opinions with fresh sets of eyes. Let them use the sample for a couple of days and then ask for feedback – constructive not destructive.

There may be something wrong, something tiny that you may not see but an "outsider" would. Get as much of this feedback as you possibly can before you go live with your product. While you are at it, check for yourself that the product does exactly what it is meant to do. This all goes towards validating, not just your product, but also your decision to choose it.

4. Use Them in Your Marketing Strategy

Your marketing strategy is vital to the success of your business and that is just what selling private label products is – a business. Take those photographs of your sample and use them, not just in your listing but also on your website, on your social network pages, anywhere you can think of to advertise. You could even make a short video of the product being demonstrated for use and then upload it. Use it on your social pages or upload to YouTube. Videos are excellent ways to tempt prospective customers because they can actually see the product being used and they can see how it works, and that it definitely does work for the purpose it is intended.

5. Test The Durability of Your Product

Push your product as far as its limits allow; make sure it is durable and doesn't break at first use. If you are advertising your product as being safe to go in the dishwasher, run your samples through the dishwasher a few times to make sure. If you say it is waterproof, put it through a few hard water tests. If the product is meant to be safe to wash and then put in a dryer, test it out, make sure it is.

You are almost trying to break your product by pushing it to its absolute limits. You have to make sure that the product works as you say it will – if you don't, you will end up with a string of bad reviews and a bad reputation.

6. Check the Specifications

Check and then double check the sample against the product specifications that supplier has given you. If the specs say that the product is 5 inches tall by 10 inches wide, and weighs 5 pounds, check that this is correct. Measure it and weigh it, make sure it the right size and weight. Check all of the specifications to make sure your product is what you – and the supplier – say it is. Your product has to match your advertisement; it is as simple as that.

7. Test, Test and Test Again

This really cannot be stressed enough: Test your sample to destruction if necessary. You need to know its durability, how far it can be pushed, how long it will last and what it can put up with. Make very sure that this product is something that you are happy to invest thousands of dollars in; a product that you know is of the quality you say it is. When you put your very first order in, you will be taking a massive risk, so make sure that it is something worth selling first.

CHAPTER SIX

LISTING YOUR PRODUCT

ON AMAZON

Amazon already has product pages for tons of products, but if your product is not in their catalogs, you can create a product page of your own. You just need to do is upload some good images of your product, write a good description for it, and give it a name. Hit save and your product page becomes visible in the Amazon catalog. However, this requires you to have a Pro Merchant account first. You don't need the Pro Merchant account to add your own listing to an existing product page.

Assuming you don't have a Pro Merchant subscription, here are the steps to do it.

1) Sign in to your Amazon Seller Central account.
2) Click on the Settings tab and then click on "Seller Account Information."
3) Click on Pro Merchant account.

4) Now click on the Inventory tab and select "Manage Your Inventory." Click on the "Create a Product Detail Page" button, which is visible only to subscribers of a Pro Merchant account.

5) You will be prompted to pick a category for your product first. Browse the available categories and select the one that you think is appropriate for your product. You can also use the search box to find a category. If there are subcategories, choose the appropriate one.

6) Type in your product's name and enter a UPC, ISBN, or any other identification code for it if you know it. This will identify your product. Fill in all the fields that have an asterisk next to them. Those are mandatory and you can't proceed further without providing that information.

7) Now write a good description for your product and upload some high-quality photos of it.

8) Once you've done that, you will be asked to enter the condition of your product, set a price for it, and enter shipping details. It's the same even if you're creating a listing for an existing product.

Most products are already available on Amazon and have a dedicated product page, so try to look for the product page first.

Check under "Find it on Amazon" and if you find a page, simply click on "Sell Yours" to create your own listing for it.

WRITE A CAPTIVATING SALES DESCRIPTION

To make a sale, you first have to sell the *idea* of your product. That's right; the first thing that needs to happen is that the customer gets interested in the idea of the product. There needs to be a desire in the mind of the buyer. Once it's there, you need to convince them that your product is the best there is. That's how a sale happens.

With Amazon, the best way you can do this is by writing a great product description. This is a tried and tested way to convince potential buyers that your product is what they need. It's very difficult for a potential customer to ignore your product if you have a product description that appeals to their psychology. So it's important for you to write a powerful product bio that gives your customers the right mental push to make them buy the product.

Let's take a look at some elements that make the product description compelling.

Address the customer

We've already said that you need to pick a product that targets a niche. The thing about niche audiences is that they are easier to appeal to because you have an idea about what they like and what they don't like. Knowing your primary customers is the most important thing for you.

If you want to sell toys for infants or very young kids, you will target women between the ages of 25-40. They're typically going to be your primary customers, so you have to write a product bio keeping them in mind. You need to directly address them in your product description.

To make it appealing to your demographic, you can do a few things. Try to make the description conversational, for a start. This makes your readers feel as if they're talking to you and that you're answering their questions instead of reading a monologue. Also, you should use the word "you" often in your description to address the buyer.

Mention the benefits, not the features

This is an elementary rule of selling anything. Don't concentrate on the features of your product, concentrate on the benefits. The buyer is not interested in knowing what the product can do; she only wants to know how the product will benefit her.

This is basic knowledge, and while it's important to do this, you need to be careful about *how* you do it, too. Start with writing down everything you know about the product. Try to be interesting; be creative and witty. It's okay to write anything good about your product, even things like the color, the material, special features, or ergonomic comfort. Once you've done this, pick the best ones and rewrite them, this time focusing on how they will benefit the user.

Technicalities

Use a few technical terms in your product description. As long as you don't go overboard, this will work in your favor and authenticate the legitimacy of your product. If you have any patents or copyrights, you should definitely mention them in the bio. It gives you and your product more credibility, and people become more inclined to buy from you.

People like unique and refined products, so mentioned any patents you have on your product at least twice. This helps to impress the customer and convince him of your product's quality.

Remember never to lie about it, however. That can quickly get you into legal trouble. So don't treat the customer like a fool, and only mention real patents and copyrights.

Impressive wording

You must weave magic with your words. Word your product description impressively, writing in a way that captures the reader's senses and persuades them into buying the product. It's not about using big words, but about writing in an impressive manner. You want the customer to feel the need to buy.

Graphic description

With online selling, you have an undeniable drawback. Your customers can't actually hold the product in their hands and check its quality. All they have are the photos of your product, so you need to make sure the photos you upload are as impressive as possible. They should be high quality with appropriate lighting, and they should also show the product from multiple angles. Be sure to highlight every physical feature of the product with all the important angles.

Accompany this with a pictographic description, talking about the details of the product in the photos and embellishing on them.

Formatting

You must have heard how important formatting is to writing good text. It makes a great deal of difference in how the customer perceives your product, so you have to pay close attention to it. Make the description as pleasant to read as possible. Here are a few tips:

- Use professional looking fonts that have appropriate spacing and no unnecessary curves. The font should look good in a sales description and shouldn't have designer elements.

- Use bullet points effectively. Put them at multiple places in the text so the reader can digest the text in small bites and get the general overview, even without reading the whole thing.

- Leave some white space between paragraphs. This makes your text more readable and easier to digest.

Highlighting

There are readers who carefully read the whole description and there are others who don't even read the bullet points properly. Sadly, there are a lot of the latter type, and this can hurt your sales if you don't allow for it. Once you've written your product description, take a look at it after a break. Mark the most important parts in it and then highlight them by making them bold and/or bigger. The point is to make them stand out so they catch the customer's attention, even if she doesn't read most of the description. This is the best way to target readers who are too impatient and to read the entire product description.

Proof

You need to give your customers some proof that people actually like using your product in order to make them believe that your product is reliable and worth its price. The best way to do this is by showing testimonials from your past customers. Put these testimonials in the product description. If you have five-star ratings and reviews, that also helps your reputation. Once the customers see the proof, they feel that your product is reliable and that they're making an informed decision when they buy it. So don't forget to provide the proof to prospective customers.

No nonsense

Don't give unnecessary information in your sales description. The customers don't need to read it, and it only adds noise to your description. Understand that people have busy lives and don't appreciate having to read unnecessary details. Remember that less is more. Revise your product description multiple times before publishing it, and take out useless information from it each time. Make sure you use impeccable grammar and spelling.

Outsourcing and supervision

If you're having it written by an outside source, make sure you supervise it. Outsourcing work isn't a bad thing, but it's important to check on the efficiency and accuracy. Read the description(s) multiple times before posting and make sure the writing is good.

CHAPTER SEVEN

SENDING THE PRODUCT FOR FBA

This chapter will discuss FBA in detail. Let's take a look at how you can use it to your advantage.

WHAT IS FBA?

FBA, or Fulfillment by Amazon, is an easy way to get your products delivered to your customers. You just have to send the products you list on the website to an Amazon warehouse, and they take it from there. Amazon gives your products more visibility, and it's an easy way to earn more. You don't have to deal with the trouble of packaging and shipping, and you get Amazon's name backing your product.

Amazon has various fulfillment centers set up at many places in the country, and all you have to do is send your inventory to these centers. You have to pay for the storage and handling of products. Whenever you receive an order, Amazon will take care of the packaging and shipping for you. When it's delivered to the customer, you'll get a notification from Amazon. Even most of the customer service is handled by Amazon if an issue arises. This helps you take your business to higher levels without putting in too much effort.

BENEFITS OF FBA

For growing sellers, FBA is really beneficial. Here are some of the main benefits of FBA:

1) Items can be shipped to customers at any time with FBA. You don't have to worry about anything related to handling, shipping, and returns. Amazon does it for you, working 24-7 to make sure your products reach the customers on time and that your customers have the best experience. You don't even have to print shipping labels for your packages. All you have to do is monitor you inventory levels so you can send in more stock when it's needed.

2) You can make use of Amazon's world-class shipping centers if you opt for FBA. Your customers get to enjoy options like low-cost shipping, free shipping, and one-day shipping without any additional headache to you, thanks to Amazon.

3) Your losses and damages are greatly reduced. This is because you're working with the most trusted e-commerce platform. Amazon's customer satisfaction rates are the highest, and they take pride in it. When you use FBA, your goods become more than your goods. They become Amazon's property for the time being, and Amazon treats them as such. Their process of order processing and inventory tracking is automated, so you don't need to worry about your merchandise getting lost or damaged. Amazon is extremely efficient.

4) Your customers are more satisfied because they get quick deliveries with great packaging.

5) You attract more buyers with FBA. This is because Amazon is a huge platform and knows well how to appeal to customers. Amazon FBA merchants enjoy greater visibility because their products are advertised to the top buyers and Amazon Prime buyers. The latter group gets a lot of offers from Amazon, and they have a much smoother buying experience, so they choose to spend much more than your average buyer.

6) Many online shoppers choose to search for relevant products directly through Amazon instead of using a search engine. This gives Amazon sellers a huge advantage over the others.

7) Once you decide on FBA, you will no longer face the limitations of a small-scale operation. You won't be crippled by poor logistics. Amazon will provide you the best logistics available, and it will level the playing field for you. This will help you grow your business rapidly and spend more time on marketing and promotional activities.

8) FBA products are the ones that are mostly advertised to the Amazon Prime members. They get exclusive discounts on these products, which boosts the sales. This is very beneficial for you and your business.

9) When you use FBA, your products get the Amazon Prime free two-day shipping option. This boosts your popularity.

10) With the multi-channel fulfillment option, you can choose to fulfill orders from other channels using the inventory you store at the Amazon centers, and you can manage your inventory online.

11) FBA offers a flexible option of pay-per-use which allows you to scale your business up or down as you wish. It has no minimum inventory item requirements nor does it have a contract or subscription fees. You have complete control over how many items you store with Amazon. You need to only pay for the storage space you use and the orders that have been fulfilled.

12) You get to spend more time developing and expanding your business because Amazon does all the shipping, promoting, and inventory work for your products. Since customers trust Amazon shipping, it will boost your sales while giving you free time to spend as you wish.

13) Amazon also handles all the customer services no matter what language they are in. They also handle the returns and ensure that you don't feel the pinch of having products returned.

How FBA Functions

Understanding FBA and its functioning is really easy. All you have to do is send your inventory to an Amazon Fulfillment Center, and from there on the Amazon people take care of it. They'll handle all the back-end operations. They do everything from storing inventory to fulfilling orders to handling customer support and order returns. They're very consistent about it, which improves your reliability as a seller. It's totally up to you how much you want to store, according to your finances.

Here's how you register for FBA:

1) Open the following URL on your web browser: www.amazon.com/fba.

2) Click on "Get Started."

3) You don't have to register for a Seller Central account since you already have one. You just have to select "Add FBA to your account".

4) Then log into your Seller Central account and check the Inventory tab.

5) Click on the "Manage Inventory" option and choose which products you would like to list for FBA. There's a checkbox next to each product and you can mark it to list it for FBA.

6) Once you've selected all the products you want to list, click on the Actions drop-down menu, and select "Change to Fulfilled by Amazon."

7) On the next page, click on "Convert."

After this, you have to ready your stock and send it to an Amazon Fulfillment Center. Here are the instructions for doing that:

1) Go to your account's Inventory tab.

2) Click on "Manage Inventory" and once again, mark the checkboxes against the items you want to go for FBA.

3) Then click on the Actions drop-down menu, and select "Send/Replenish Inventory."

4) Then you'll be asked to give a ship address. Provide the necessary details.

5) You will be asked how you're going to ship the products: case-packed or individual items.

Note: Before you do this, make sure to take a look at the Dangerous Units, Hazardous Materials, and EBA Prohibited Products page, to be sure everything is legal.

The next step is to review the labeling requirements. Amazon's receiving systems are dependent on barcodes; so all units you send to them must be tagged with a barcode that is able to be scanned. There are three ways to do this:

1) Manually print and apply labels to each unit.
2) Use the Label Service from FBA itself. Everything will be handled by Amazon.
3) If your products are eligible, sign up for the Stickerless Commingled Inventory.

Here are Amazon's recommendations for when you are preparing to print labels for your products:

- Use a laser or a thermal printer and avoid inkjet printers. This will decrease chances of fading and smearing.

- Your printer should be able to handle resolutions above 300DPI.

- Make sure you're using the right print media.

- Regularly clean and replace your printer heads.

- Test your labels periodically by scanning them yourself. See if they're legible.

You will receive a PDF file once you have entered the number of units you'll be shipping for each product. You can print these labels later. Again, there are some guidelines:

- Use white label stock with removable adhesive to print the labels. This makes them easily scannable and removable.

- Make sure only product label that Amazon provided is visible. If there are other barcodes on your product/package, hide them all properly.

- Some products require prepping before they are shipped, which can slow down the shipping process. To avoid this, you can use FBA Prep Services. You can also send them fully prepped to the fulfillment centers.

- Each box sent to Amazon should have a unique shipping label. It's the only way to identify it at the fulfillment center.

Here are your guidelines for attaching the labels:

- Don't place the labels on a place where they'll be cut. Try to place them in the middle of the box if possible. Never place them on the seams or corners.

- There must be a unique shipping label on each box.

- If there are pallets, each one has to have five labels. One goes on the top and the others go on each side.

When all of this is done, schedule a time for the pickup of your inventory. Mark all the items you are shipping as "Shipped" in the Shipment Summary. From there on, you can track the status of your shipment in the Shipping Queue. Allow a period of at least 24 hours before checking whether the status is updated to "Delivered." After that, you can contact your carrier to confirm delivery.

"Checked-In" means that some part of your shipment has reached, and they're waiting for the rest. Once the barcode scanning starts; the status again changes to "Receiving." The whole process usually takes about six days, so be patient. After this, the dimensions of all your products are recorded. Once they're stored, they can be shipped anytime.

Amazon's web-to-warehouse picking system is very advanced. It can sort through inventories in the warehouse really fast and when a customer purchases something, it will pick the right method of shipping them the product according to their preference. The order can be accurately tracked by the customer throughout the shipping process. This makes for a very pleasant experience for the customer.

HOW TO GET PAID WITH FBA

Getting paid with FBA is super simple. You can check the status of your orders at any time by going to the "Manage Orders" page in your Amazon Seller Central account. It will show either of these two: "Payment Complete" or "Pending." If you go to the "Reports" tab, you can check whether you have actually received the payment for the order. There will be a transaction for every order.

Is FBA worth it?

This question does not have one answer. Whether FBA is worth your time depends on a large number of factors. FBA might not be worth it for every seller. In this section we shall talk about how to judge if FBA is THE option for your business.

1. Size and Price

The first thing you should consider is the size and price of your product. The handling and packing fees are fixed on FBA but the fees changes according to weight and size of your items.

Essentially, if your product is small, light-weight and pricey, the FBA fees seem very reasonable. For example, if you have a $20 item that is big and heavy, then you would be spending a large amount of your price on the FBA fees. However, if your item is small and light-weight and has a price of $50, you would spend very little of your price margin on the FBA fees. Hence, you need to judge if the amount you spend on FBA is worth signing up for it.

Also, if your product is a popular one, then the chances of selling large numbers of it are very high. It doesn't make sense to use FBA to sell slow-moving items since you would be spending a ton of money on storage fees. However, the other side to using FBA to sell slow-moving items is that the "fulfilled" status might give the items the momentum they need to sell.

2. *Number of items*

If you were a big seller with a large number of items then, finding and paying for storage space on your own would be incredibly expensive. Hence, it makes sense to use Amazon's FBA to store your products since there is no drawback to joining FBA. Your sales could increase and you could store your items for a cheaper fee than anywhere else.

If you are a small business that wants to expand, you could use FBA as a way of decreasing your workload by allowing Amazon to store and ship your products. This gives you enough time to plan on expanding your business.

3. *Manpower*

If you lack the manpower to cope with a large number of orders, FBA is the option for you. If you run your business by yourself, it seems impractical for you to pack and take each item to the post office. People are willing to pay for fast shipping and they do not want to wait for days to receive the product. You need to be able to dispatch their orders almost immediately. If you get bulk orders, this might be difficult. You could take on employees, but that could be an additional burden to you since you would have to manage them, pay them, and deal with their problems.

It will also be difficult to judge the time when you get an influx of orders unless your products are restricted to a particular season. Even then it is hard to predict flux and hence difficult to hire employees in time to deal with that.

To prevent all these messy problems, it might work out easier for you to sign up for FBA since they take the huge burden of shipping off your shoulders.

4. *Your opinion of Amazon's reputation*

At the end of the day, there are success stories both from people who have used FBA and those who haven't. There are some people who steadfastly believe in running their business by themselves and not trusting any outside source, that is, Amazon or another such company that offers to ship their products or take care of part of the business. However, there are some proven benefits of using FBA. The tag that you get as an FBA seller gives the customer the same trust in you that they have in Amazon. Reputation always matters. Also, FBA sellers can make more money because they can sell for more. For example, if you sell a pack of 4 bottles for $40 with a shipping rate of $10, you would have to go to the post office to send out your item. Hence, the $10 goes for the post office trip and the shipping cost. However, by using FBA you could charge the same $50 but instead of spending the $10 for shipping, you can add that to your profit. The cost remains the same to the customer but you get more profit out of it.

The Ultimate Toolkit to be a Successful FBA Seller

To be the best in your craft you need to be able to utilize your tools in the best way possible. This applies for an Amazon seller as well. You need to make sure you have your equipment ready before you decide to become an Amazon FBA seller. These tools will be essential in setting up your FBA business and ensuring that you become a successful FBA seller.

Smartphone

A smartphone is a necessity in today's business world, not a luxury. It is the one tool that will allow you to actively control all aspects of your business. However, if you feel that a smartphone might spoil your life, then a computer with a decent Internet connection is the only other option. As you expand your business, a smartphone would be most useful since it would allow you to control your business even on the go. It gives you a lot of flexibility and space to work from wherever you feel comfortable.

Scouting apps

Scouting apps are extremely useful when it comes to building up your business. These apps are easily available on your smartphones.

Good printer

A good quality inkjet printer is a must with a constant stock of A4 or letter-sized sheets of paper. If you can manage to get a laser or thermal printer, it's even better because the printing will not fade.

Packing equipment

This is the most important part of the toolkit. As a seller, you should never have a shortage of packing materials. Make sure you have more than the necessary number of cartons, bubble wrap, boxes, covers, labels, tape, and other essential packing items. Cutters, scissors, tapes, and wrapping paper or covers play a major role in the packing of your products, especially those that need to be gift wrapped. You will also need tools to remove the stickers put on the product by the manufacturers.

Guidelines to Efficient and Proper Packing

When you choose FBA for your products, it will be a definite boost for your business. However, before you get ready to sell to your products and increase your profit, you need to focus on how you package your products for delivery to the Amazon Fulfillment Centers. The easiest way to do that would be to follow Amazon's rules on packaging. They have certain rules and guidelines based on the kind of item you plan to sell. The Amazon help section will provide you with a comprehensive list of guidelines to follow. However, here is a list of guidelines that aren't often mentioned for some popular products. These guidelines will help you ensure that your product reaches Amazon safely and also that Amazon doesn't reject the product based on its packaging—or lack of it.

Adult section

This section is the one that contains nude photos, sex toys or obscene material. They need to be packed only in a black bag or opaque bag. This is a specific criterion for these products. There should also be a suffocation warning pasted on the top. Most importantly, it should not contain any product information. There should be no label regarding what the product is.

Apparel and toys

For items that fall in the apparel and toys category, it is enough if you use simple, translucent packing with a label containing suffocation or hazardous parts warning on it. Also the bag or cover should be strong enough to protect the item from dirt and dust.

Electronic gadgets and equipment

These items are usually sturdy and do not need any bubble wrap. A simple packaging in a bag with a hazardous of suffocation label will be enough for these products.

Fragile products

Fragile products are those that require the most care. They need the most secure and finest packing. For example, if you are selling a glass product, you need to wrap at least two or three layers of bubble wrap around it, followed by a cover and finally a box. Your product will need to pass a drop test before it is cleared by Amazon.

Gifts

Even though Amazon's FBA service comes with a gift-wrap option for the orders, it is always better if you send them a note indicating which items are gifts and which aren't. This makes it easier for Amazon to dispatch the items. You also have to remove all the manufacturer's stickers from the product before you send to Amazon. The barcode for each of your products should be accessible easily. The scanning for the barcode is usually done on top of the package, so it is essential that you put the barcode label on the top and not anywhere on the sides or the seams. Also, it should always be on the packaging and not on the product itself because then that defies the purpose of you packaging the product.

Liquids

A liquid product needs to have a double seal. You have to make sure it doesn't leak; Amazon will not do a drop test to check the packaging's strength, as that would compromise the product.

Set packs

Most sellers sell their books or stationary or movie CDs as a set pack. These packs will be a compilation of similar works or all the books in a series or a box full of similar stationary items. While packaging these products, you need to be very careful if there is no stacking unit. If you do not have a common predesigned box for your set pack, then it is useful if you can put all the items in a single carton or box and label it as a set. When you do so, you are clearly informing Amazon that these items need to be shipped as one, even though they do not come in a single box from the manufacturer. Sticking a "sold as a set" label on the top of the box will help Amazon identify that needs to be sold as a whole.

Tools

These items need at least a layer of bubble wrap around them as a precaution. This ensures that they do not cause any harm during transport or delivery.

CHAPTER EIGHT

AMAZON PAY PER CLICK ADVERTISING

Amazon has one of the world's largest e-commerce search engines. Customers perform millions of searches on Amazon's search engine. Amazon leads their customers to the best product related to their search. Just like Google, Amazon also sells some space on its website to the highest bidder. This allows Amazon to make some extra money and it also allows sellers to advertise their products.

The more people who see your product, the more items you are likely to sell. The more people use the keywords related to your product, the more likely they are to find your product. A lot of sellers do not make use of this feature solely because they have to pay a small amount for it. However, for that small investment the outcome can be large and much more profitable for you, as a seller.

These ads are known as "Pay Per Click" ads. Basically, you pay only when people click on your advertisement. Amazon sets out a bid for the spaces they allot for advertisements and sell each to the highest bidder. Usually, this is about $1 for each time a person clicks on your advertisement.

Let's see how you can bid for these slots to improve your sales.

Step 1

The very first thing you need to do is to prepare your list of products. You need to make sure that this list is accurate. There is no use paying for advertisements that link to a page that has low-resolution images or lacks crucial information. As with any e-commerce business, make sure that your product pages are easy to understand, full of information, and memorable. Your aim is to sell your product to your visitors via your words and images. Remember to get some reviews before you pay for your product to appear of Amazon's Pay Per Click slot because customers tend to distrust products that do not have any reviews on them. Finally, make sure that all the keywords you used, the main ones, are mentioned in your listing.

Step 2

There are two kinds of ads to choose from. One is an Amazon Product ad, which sends visitors to your own business website; the other is an Amazon Sponsored Products ad, which sends the visitors to your products on Amazon. In this section we will go over Amazon Sponsored Ads. You get twice the exposure with these kinds of ads because they highlight your product in the internal search engines.

Step 3

Go to the advertising tab in the Seller Central section and click on the Campaign Manager option.

Step 4

That takes you to a page where you can select the option of "Create ad campaign" to start advertising. The best part of the Pay Per Click ads on Amazon is that the first $50 worth of ads is completely free.

Step 5

Click on "Create ad campaign" takes you to a page where you can add parameters to your advertisement.

Your campaign name: You need to select a name for your campaign so that it is easy for you to identify it at some given point. Be specific with the name you give. If you plan to add a wide range of products, then at some point you are going to have a large number of campaigns, hence a specific name will make it easier for you to identify the campaign.

Average daily budget: You need to also specify how much you are willing to spend per day. The minimum average you can spend is $1. If you are new to this, I would suggest that you start with $1 and work your way up as your confidence and revenue build.

Start date: You need to select a start date. Ideally, pick a date as close to the current date as possible.

End date: You can also choose when you want Amazon to stop putting up your products as ads on the website. Ideally, do not pick an end date before you start. You can add an end date later on.

Targeting type: There are two targeting type that you can choose from. One is automatic targeting and the other is manual targeting. If you are new to the whole Pay Per Click advertising concept, I would suggest that you choose automatic targeting. Manual targeting gives you more control over your target audience but automatic makes it easier if you are just trying to learn how to use Pay Per click ads. Automatic Targeting can sometimes be bad at generating profitable ads so weigh your pros and cons before making a decision. However, initially you can use it as a way to pick Amazon's brains as to how to find new keywords. You can sometimes find some really useful keywords using the automatic targeting option.

A lot of people use the advertisements just to check which keywords they need to target. It can be a great way to figure out which keywords are going to convert the best. You can use automatic targeting to figure out the keywords. Then do an analysis of the keywords to determine which bring you the best profits.

If you are already good at this, or already have a list of target keywords, then it might be better to use manual targeting. It works better in the long run because automatic targeting will only turn out to be more expensive for any use other than to discover keywords.

Once you have entered in all the information, click on "Continue."

Step 6

You will then get to a page that will allow you to name the ads and select the products that you want to advertise.

Name the ad group: You can just use the same title as your campaign name if you want.

Default bid: You can set a default bid amount every time bidding opens. Since the minimum is $0.05, you can use that as the default unless it doesn't work, in which case you can increase it a bit.

Select products: You can choose which of the products from your inventory you can run ads for. You can add as few or as many products as you like.

Finally, click "Save and finish."

Step 7

Now you have to wait for your campaigns to begin working. It would be unrealistic for you to expect your campaigns to work immediately. It is very rare for campaigns to be profitable in the first few weeks or even first few months. You need to give your campaigns some time, unlike those on Adwords or Facebook. This is because Amazon tends to reduce the cost per click over time and the Pay Per Click influences your organic rankings. Your conversion rates also increase over a span of time rather than immediately. So you need to have some patience before you decide to give up on your campaign.

While some advertisement campaigns are instant winners, most of them are initially losers but pick up after a week or two. The bottom line is that you shouldn't be in a hurry to turn off a campaign until you have given it sufficient time to prove that it can be a winner.

A few points to remember about Amazon's Pay Per Click advertising:

- The ads run only when your item has the "Buy Box" option. This allows you to save money by not running ads when your item isn't in the popular list.

- You can start and stop your campaign whenever you feel like it.

- You will see an amazing improvement in sales once your items get advertised on the website.

- When you run ads, the visitors to your product pages increase and with that your sales will increase. An increase in sales automatically leads to a better organic rank, which is worth more than you pay for your ads.

CHAPTER NINE

BRAND PROMOTION

Creating your own brand is essential for a number of reasons. If you want to become a top seller on Amazon, you have to create your own brand identity. Your product needs to have a unique identity that is relatable to customers. This, combined with quality services, will inspire loyalty among your customers, and they'll keep coming back to buy from you. You should distinguish your product from others in the market by making small changes to it and customizing it. This also helps you get more orders and advance to become a top seller.

How you choose to brand your product depends a lot on what kind of product you are selling. For some products, it may be as easy as sticking a label on the product. For others, you might have to make more efforts, like getting a logo etched onto the product during the manufacturing process itself. You can create a unique box for some. It's also an easy way to differentiate your product. There are many other ways to do it. You just have to get creative and use it to your advantage. Create a custom pack for your product, maybe. If others sell in packs of 100 ounces, you could sell in packs of 150 ounces. People might just like the larger size.

You can also add a hand-made card in your product package. This helps in emotional bonding with the customer because of the personal touch and the sense of uniqueness.

You can do a lot of things to promote your brand. Start a blog or a website for the product and divert traffic to the Amazon site. You can even embed an e-store in your website, so you can directly sell from there. You can also make people sign up for your newsletter. If it's interesting, people will leave you their email addresses, which you can use for promotional purposes.

Here are some things to get you in the right mindset for promotion:

- Branding is not an unnecessary cost. It's an investment that helps you sell more.

- When starting out, avoid spending large amounts on promotion.

- When deciding on a brand name and a logo, consider what your customers like, not what you like. Do solid research to come up with the right name and logo.

- Make sure your logo looks polished and professionally designed. Amateurish logos send the wrong signals.

- If all your products cater to the same audience, keep them under the same brand. If they belong to different niches, it's better to brand them separately.

If you want to create a serious business, branding is very important for you. You will only notice its impact in the long term. It's okay to not brand all of your products in the beginning. Do it with one product and once you're making consistent profits, brand other products, too.

Once there's a name for your brand in the market, you should start promoting it if you have enough profits. Start advertising your product by using PPC (Pay Per Click), SEO (Search Engine Optimization), and other techniques. Today, there are a lot of ways to advertise.

You should also consider services such as "Amazon Product Ads." Amazon will create custom ads for you and target the right customers. You'll be charged on a PPC basis, just like other services. Google Adwords is also a great PPC service.

"Amazon Webstore Service" is a quick way to create a professional looking website for your products. It's linked to your Seller Central account, so you can get full integration with all the services and tools you use on Amazon.

BECOMING A TOP SELLER

There are too many sellers in the market for almost any product. Getting customers' attention is hard because of the competition. So how do you get an edge?

For this, you have to understand Amazon's "buy box" algorithm first. This algorithm decides which seller gets the first right to sell if a customer directly clicks on "Add to card" after searching for a product. The seller who wins the buy box is called the top seller. The customers can choose to look for other sellers but, in most cases, they don't. They simply buy from the default seller.

Some sellers may be near the customer, and some may be selling more customized items. Others could be offering lower prices or shipping costs, and yet others may be providing unique value-added services. Most buyers, however, don't bother looking for different sellers. So the "buy box" seller automatically sells the most.

Creating a brand identity gives you the golden opportunity to win the "buy box." You have to invest more in marketing, but it's very beneficial in the long run. Winning the buy box gives you sales a huge boost, so always go for custom branding when you can.

Here are some tips to become a top seller on Amazon.

Quality products

Always sell high-quality products. It's the best way to get a good rating for your product. Cheap knock-offs will never be a top product, even if you profit in the short run. Satisfy your customer with great products and they'll give you good reviews to build your reputation.

Timely shipping

Once you receive an order, ship the product as soon as possible. Customers loathe late deliveries, so if you want them to come back, don't give them a sour experience. *Always* ship on time.

Fair prices

Don't mark up your products too high. You may make big profits at first, but your sales volume will suffer. To become a top seller, cut your profit margins a bit, because low prices attract customers.

Customer satisfaction

Getting good customer reviews requires keeping customers happy, and that takes work. It's important for you to maintain good product rating, because even a single negative review will impact your sales greatly in the beginning. Always deal with your customers calmly and pleasantly, and use an email auto-responder to shoot quick first responses to customer emails.

High-quality photos

Always use high-quality photos for your products and make sure you capture it from a variety of angles. Customers need to get a good feel for it before they buy it. If you can't take professional photos for your product, hire a photographer to get it done.

Product descriptions

As we have already discussed, writing compelling product descriptions is very important. It gives your potential customers a push and converts them into actual customers. Write detailed descriptions for your products and make them customer-oriented.

Dealing with complaints

The customers at Amazon don't hesitate to file a complaint if they are unsatisfied with their experience, and Amazon is the king of customer service. So make sure you deal with all your customer complaints quickly and reasonably. Amazon always looks at the situation without any bias, so you should be in the clear. Always satisfy your customers and your ratings will stay high.

Everything you do is just a means to an end here, the end being positive customer reviews. That's the biggest factor in determining your seller rank. You might hear about people using gray-market techniques like paid reviews. I strongly advise you against it. If caught, your Amazon account may be terminated and the business you built with so much hard work will collapse in seconds. Honesty on your part is of utmost importance.

Sometimes, it will be impossible to become a top seller, and that's okay. It just means that your niche is too competitive and you need to switch to a less competitive one to become a top seller.

THE IMPORTANCE OF BUILDING AN EMAIL LIST

One of the best ways to advertise your products is through your own website and, providing it is a good one, you will be able to direct more traffic than you ever dreamed possible, not just to your website but on to your Amazon product page as well. This is even more important if you have more than one product for sale.

The Amazon FBA niche has got everything you want – an audience that is obsessive about buying products, social media sites at your disposal, blogs and forums that are ideal for reaching your target audience. You get to drive traffic to your website and your page by commenting on blog posts and on forums. You can set up a Facebook page or Twitter account and do the same thing, or comment on other pages that are related and influential.

You can go to other blogs for Amazon FBA and get some ideas for content on your blog, then write it much bigger, much better, and much bolder to make sure you stand out. Provided you do this right, your audience will grow and so will your profits. By getting together with others in this niche and networking, you can share their content, link to their blog and watch your own website grow – and most will return the favor.

One of the most important things that you must do before you begin with your Amazon FBA product is build up an email list. These are people that you can legally target with information about your product and you can build up a strong rapport with them and watch them spread the word for you. This is one of the biggest and most important elements in promoting your business.

How to get started

To begin with, you need:

- A good website. You can start with a free one or you can pay for one. Make sure that it looks professional and that your content is relevant and kept up to date – post regularly. The best type of website to start with is a blog and you can do that with a free WordPress account

- A good reliable web host. The free ones offer a host but you are better off searching for one that is reliable

- A good domain name that is brandable

- A good premium WordPress or StudioPress theme

- Good images and photos – either take your own or use royalty-free images. If you want to use those that are not royalty free, you will need either to contact the owner for permission or purchase the image.

- A good auto-responder to help you to build up your email list and to keep in touch with your customers

- A good email capture tool to help you to grow your email list very quickly

If you are really serious about building up your business, your biggest priority is to build up a big healthy email list. This is the one asset that you have total control over and one of the best ways to start is by having a good presence on social media. You should also aim for a high ranking on the search engines, particularly Google. However, both of these require you to stay up to date with the changes in algorithms that Google and Facebook are constantly bringing in. Your email list is different – that is yours; nobody can take it away from you and nobody can change it.

You must use your website and your social media pages to attract attention, to tempt people to visit your site and to follow you. You need to encourage them to fill in your opt-in form and sign up for your email list. Once they have done this, you can contact them by email, because they have given you permission to do so – do be careful not to flood their inboxes with too much though; even though they have signed up, this can still be considered spam and it can earn a very serious black mark against your name.

GETTING STARTED – THE BASICS OF BUILDING AN EMAIL LIST

To start building a decent email list, one that you can use to promote your Amazon FBA products, there are several things you need to do. The following list covers the absolute basic tasks you must do to stand any chance of success:

- *Find a good email marketing service*

And sign up for it. Because we are starting right at the very beginning, I will assume that you have not yet got an email service provider. This will give you all of the tools that you need, the templates to use and the services that are vital to getting you the right subscribers, to test out your sales and marketing campaign and to manage all of the daily tasks that your list requires.

There are a lot of email service providers to choose from and each will have a different pricing model. It is important that you do your research carefully and choose the right service for the list size you want to build and the growth that you intend to happen. Some service providers charge a flat fee every month, based on the size of your list, and others will charge you for the amount of emails that are sent. One of the best free services to use when you are starting out is MailChimp.

- *Come up with the right temptation*

Before anyone gives you their email address, they will want something for it. You have to come up with the right offer that will tempt them to sign up for your email list. This could be a free gift, an eBook, access to a hot webinar, discounts—anything that is tempting enough to reel them in. You could rewrite a couple of pieces of your content, turning them into how-to guides or resources lists. Whatever you do, whatever offer you make, it has to be compelling and it has to be something that is seen as having an actual value.

- *Create your opt-in form*

No matter which email service provider you choose, it will provide you with all the tools you need to create your opt-in form to go on your website. In general, you should keep it to basics; ask for the minimum amount of information, such as first name and email address only. Your prospect is far more likely to sign up if you are not asking for reams of or probing information. Obviously, you need their email address and just asking for their first name means that you can send personalized emails and offers to them. If you ask for more information than this, your chances of conversion will drop rapidly and you will not gain any valuable information.

- *Insert the opt-in form on your website*

This is relatively easy to do and normally involves nothing more than copying a piece of code, provided by your service provider, and then pasting it to your website. Placement of the form is important – you want it where it can be seen but not so that it overpowers the rest of your content. Most people tend to put it in the right hand sidebar, a place that has been proven to have the highest conversion rate. However, you can place it anywhere you like and the seven best and highest converting places on your website are:

- In a special feature box

- At the very top of the sidebar

- At the end of each piece of content or blog post

- In the footer of your website

- On your About Us or Contact Us Page

- Across the top of the page in a little bar. WordPress contains plugins that can help you with this

- In a box that pops up

Each of these places will perform in a different way, depending on your audience, the niche you are in, and your website. Test out lots of different locations to see what pulls in the most sign-ups.

Do make sure that you provide new subscribers to your list with easy access to the offer you are using to tempt them into signing up. If it is an eBook, a webinar, or another piece of content, give them a download link on the page that they will be sent to when they have confirmed their email address to you. If it is a discount off a purchase, make sure you provide them with the relevant code or details that they need to claim the discount.

THE NEXT STEP – GETTING PEOPLE TO SUBSCRIBE

Now that you have yourself set up to collect email addresses, the hard part starts. If you already get a reasonable amount of traffic to your website and you have something to offer that cannot be missed, it shouldn't be very difficult to get people to subscribe. However, most people will need to start looking outside of their existing audience to build up an email list. The following are the best ways to get people to subscribe to your list:

- *Utilize lists from other people*

Consider offering something to someone else who will plug your business on his or her website. It needs to be something that the other person wants, even if it is a return, i.e., you plugging them on your site. You can also approach someone and suggest a joint venture. You will not be able plug them in your newsletter but you can use other avenues for promotion – your website if you already get good levels of traffic, your social media accounts, etc.

- *Add your opt-in form to another form*

There is a good chance that your website already contains forms, such as registrations, contact forms for requesting quotes, entries to contests, etc. If your site has any forms already, you can add an opt-in box. This is a fantastic and easy way to build up your email list because your visitors are already clearly interested in what you are offering.

- *Have a contest or a giveaway*

If you do these right, giveaways and contests can be an excellent way of bringing in new, highly-targeted leads. This will work better if you already have a good audience on your social media accounts but you can bring in entrants in other ways as well.

The best way is to offer a giveaway of something that is very valuable to your target audience. You can give away or offer the chance to win products that are related to your niche, but be careful that you are not attracting people who are interested only in the prize, not the rest of what you have to offer.

These are some of the very best ways to attract people to your site and fill in your opt-in form. Don't be disappointed if something doesn't work; find another way. There are plenty of things to try, just don't try them all at once. Slow and steady really does win the race here; trying to do too much will only ensure that you crash and burn.

CHAPTER TEN

AMAZON FEES – IS THE COST WORTH IT?

Amazon is one of the largest online marketplaces in the world.

They sell in more than 13 different countries and have more than 80 fulfillment centers across the world. Each day, millions of sellers sell millions of products. If you are an online seller, the chances are you will most definitely benefit from selling on Amazon but you do need to understand the costs involved. You already know about the costs of buying your merchandise and your shipping options and costs, but what about the fees that Amazon charges you?

HOW MUCH DOES IT COST?

The fees that you will be charged to sell on Amazon will depend on the selling program that you opt for and the category of the product that you sell. Amazon charges all retailers a "referral" fee, and a "variable closing" fee, taken from your sale price. Be aware that the sale price they use includes the cost of shipping and gift-wrapping. Below are the fees that you can expect to pay to sell your products on Amazon.com.

All sellers are charged a percentage of every sale, although listing your product is free:

Seller Fees	Individual Seller	Pro Merchant
Flat Fee	$0.99 per item in addition to the % fee	$39.99 per month but no $0.99 fee per item
Sales Percentage Fee	Variable, depending on product category	Variable, depend on product category

If you have a large business and you sell 40 or more products every month, then it will pay you to be enrolled in the Pro Merchant program.

REFERRAL FEE

The referral fee is the figure that Amazon will charge you per sale and is determined by the company's CPA – Cost per Acquisition model and their inventory model. These are the fees by category:

Category	Referral Fee %	Minimum Referral Fee %
Amazon Kindle, Baby Products (Not Baby clothing), Beauty, Books, Clothing & Accessories, Health & Personal Care, Home & Garden, Kitchen, Luggage & Travel, Music, Musical Instruments, Office Products, Outdoors, Shoes, Handbags & Sunglasses, Software & Computer/ Video, games, Toys & Games, Videos & DVD, Video Games, Watches, Other	15%	$1 Not applicable for Videos, DVDs, Kindle Books, video game or software $2 for watches

Automotive & Power ports, Industrial & Scientific, Tools & Home Improvement	12% Not for wheels or tires	$1
Camera & Photo, Consumer Electronics, Unlocked Cell Phones, Video game Consoles	8%	$1 Not applicable to video game consoles
Collectible Coins, Electronic Accessories, Entertainment Collectibles, Major Appliances, Sports Collectibles	Variable	$1
Jewelry	20%	$2
Accessories for Kindle	25%	Not Applicable
Personal Computers	6%	$1

Amazon will charge the buyer the cost of the product, the shipping fees, and any other fees, such as for gift wrap, that are applicable to the sale. The seller is given a percentage of this amount, less any fees for referral, and seller account fees.

AMAZON FBA AND SELLING ON AMAZON

If you use Amazon FBA to sell on Amazon, you will send your merchandise to Amazon and then sell the products on your listing page. Under Fulfillment by Amazon, all your goods are sorted and packaged by Amazon and then shipped.

If you choose to use FBA, you can expect to pay between 8 and 15% of the sale price per item as well as your FBA fees, while Selling on Amazon sellers will be charged a referral fee. You will also be charged storage fees if you use FBA.

Fees	Sell on Amazon FBA	Sell on Amazon
CPA fees	8-15% - depends on your product category	8-15%, depending on product category
Handling the Order	Media items - $0 Non-media items - $1	

	Clothing - $1 + weight handling*	
Pick and Pack	Media - $1.02 Non-media - $1.02 Clothing - $1.42 + weight handling*	
Storage Feed	January to September – $0.51 per cubic foot for standard sized, $0.40 per cubic foot for oversized October to December - $0.68 per cubic foot for standard, $0.53 per cubic foot for oversized	
Inventory Placement Service Fee	Standard – up to 2 lb. - $0.30 - $0.40 Between 2 lb. and 5 lb. - $0.30 - $0.40 plus $0.10 per	

	pound	
	Oversized – 5 lb. and over - $1.30 plus $0.50 per pound over 5 lb.	

* Based on the outbound shipping weight; fees will also vary depending on the size of the product

More details can be found on the relevant pages on Amazon.com but this should give you an idea of the fees you can expect to pay. With all of this information to hand, you can now decide if you think using Amazon or Amazon FBA is worth it for you.

CHAPTER ELEVEN

MARKETING STRATEGIES

There are a number of ways in which you can market your products. This chapter will look exclusively at the ways of marketing your products on other websites. As with any kind of marketing, the page that depicts your product is designed so that customers will feel inclined to buy your products. You will need to upload high-resolution images and create listings that draw in customers and contain detailed descriptions.

Let's have a look at some of the most popular online marketing platforms.

GOOGLE

Google is the most used search engine, so it is no surprise that this is one of the most popular online marketing platforms.

Besides its search engines, Google has a whole host of other features that you can use to market your products.

Here is a brief description of all the features that Google has at your disposal to help market your business.

Google My Business

Google My Business is a way for you to advertise your business for free on Google. You can use this tool to manage how your business appears to Google users across the world in the search bar as well as on maps. You can also use it as a way to interact with customers. While Google My Business does not directly affect your Amazon marketing, it is still a useful way to direct more customers to your products.

It allows you to manage the online presence of your business. By using this to verify your business online, you can connect to customers by helping them find you.

Google My Business offers you a number of features and benefits:

Managing your information

You can manage information that Google users will see across the world. If you verify your business, users are more likely to trust your business, since it has been endorsed by Google. Make sure you have information such as addresses, contact numbers, website links, and working hours available for potential customers to see easily.

Customer interaction

Once you verify your business, Google will allow customers to review and rate your business. You can use these reviews as a way to interact with your customers. Businesses who add images to their listings attract more customers and more visits to their websites from Google than those that don't.

Expand your presence on the Internet

You can look up how your customers arrived at your website or product listing on Amazon. You can also see which areas these people are coming from. You can use this information to modify and improve your listings, website, and product descriptions. You can even check how many of your customers called your business address directly from the phone numbers on the search results.

The best part of Google My Business is the fact that it is completely free.

Google+ Page

A Google+ page is something you get automatically once you verify your business on Google My Business. While a lot of people maintain a Google+ page is a waste of time since it isn't a priority in search engine results, it is better for local businesses to play it safe and maintain a Google+ page. Since you have verified your business, customers will be linked to your Google+ page and that makes it essential for you to maintain your Google+ page.

If your customers seem to be active on Google+, then it might be a good idea for you to add a Google+ share button on your website (if you have one).

Google Webmaster Tools

Google Webmaster Tools will provide you with alerts to any possible danger signs that could prevent your product from being displayed in search engine results. It can also help you analyze the existing traffic to help you see how people are directed to your product listing on Amazon or your website. You just need to set up a Google Webmaster Tools account in order to use the features provided by this tool.

Google AdWords

Google AdWords works along the same lines as Amazon's Pay Per Click advertisements, helping you increase your organic rank once you start using AdWords. Basically, just as with Amazon, you create ads that use specific target keywords related to your products. Your ads will appear at the top or on the right hand side of search engine results on Google. Your ads will appear only when people search for the keywords mentioned in your ads. You will be charged only when someone clicks on your ad and not for how long the ad runs. However, what you pay when someone clicks on your ad depends on the demand for the target keywords you use. If you use AdWords smartly, you can plan your strategy keeping AdWords in mind. AdWords becomes expensive in the long run. It is a quick and short-term solution rather than a long-term one. You can use it to analyze which keywords get you better results; that is pretty much what Amazon Pay Per Click advertisements do, but AdWords are on a bigger platform.

Google AdWords Keywords Planner

If you plan to improve your Search Engine Optimization, you need to do some keyword research beforehand. Keyword research will help you identify the keywords that target your specific product. It will allow you to optimize and the keywords that you use to direct traffic towards your products. The Google AdWords Keyword Planner was initially designed as a tool to help plan out your AdWords campaign. However, it can also help you get ideas for new keywords and provide you with suggestions or tips to improve your organic keyword research. While this will prove useful, keep in mind that you need to set up an AdWords account before you can use the Google AdWords Keyword Planner. However, just because you create the account doesn't necessarily mean that you have to create an ad campaign.

Google Trends

Like Google AdWords Keyword Planner, Google Trends is a great tool that will help you choose better keywords. It allows you to evaluate the popularity of keywords. You can also compare keywords and analyze how the popularity varies over time and in different parts of the world. It even shows you related keywords.

This is particularly useful when you have a large number of keywords and do not how to shorten the list. You can just do a quick comparison on Google Trends to see which ones are more popular and set those as your keywords.

Google Trends is also useful in identifying news, content, and topics.

Google Alerts

Google Alerts allows you to keep an eye on web traffic for specific phrases and keywords. Once you enable this tool, you will receive an email or RSS results whenever somebody looks up the keywords or phrases mentioned. For example, you can sign up to receive notifications when people mention your products or your company. You can even set it up to send you notifications when people search for your competitors so that you can gauge whether you have an upper hand or not. This tool is an amazing way to keep an eye on the reputation of your business and react to any online chatter immediately and improve your standing.

Google Analytics

Google Analytics is the perfect tool for studying your business. With it, you can analyze how many of your visitors are new ones and how long they spend looking at your products or site. The best part of this tool is the fact that it is absolutely free. It gives a deeper look into website traffic and helps you figure out how people are arriving at your product list so that you can figure out a way to optimize that route and make more people turn up at your product listings.

However, you cannot use this tool as a substitute for your market analysis. You will still need to do market analysis but you can use this tool as an aid in tracking your visitors all the way from when they arrive as viewers to when they leave as customers.

Google FeedBurner

If you plan to extend your reach, then Google FeedBurner is your tool. To extend your reach you should allow visitors to subscribe to your site or lead them from your products on Amazon to your website or to your blog. You can achieve this by setting up a Google FeedBurner account. Once you set up this account, your visitors will be allowed to subscribe to your content and you can provide them with regular updates via email, RSS readers, or browsers. Since subscribers play a major role in deciding the growth of a website, it is essential that you use this tool to help you gain more subscribers.

FACEBOOK

Facebook is the most popular social networking platform. It has more than a billion active users, which is more than the population of many countries. By using Facebook ads, you have the potential to reach a huge number of possible customers. It gives you an opportunity to promote your products. A large number of e-commerce businesses have managed to grow into large business because of successful Facebook marketing.

The very first thought that comes to your mind when you think of advertising on Facebook, especially if you own a small business, may be that the advertising could cost too much.

Another worry might be that it is too early in your business life for you to spend on advertising. In this section you will get to know about the basics of advertising on Facebook. Hopefully by the end of it you will have an idea of what goes into a Facebook ad and you can gauge if you should spend money on it.

Who can create Facebook ads?

Anybody who has a Facebook account can create an advertisement. However, to get the most out of Facebook advertising, it is better if you first start a Facebook page for your business before advertising your products. This will help the viewers attach a company to the product. It also gives you more flexibility when creating the advertisement.

Why should you create Facebook ads?

The reason Facebook ads are popular is because of their high specificity. You can make the target of your ads as specific as you wish. Facebook collects an enormous amount of data from its users that make it easier for you to target a specific portion of the population. For example, you can sell an anti-ageing cream to 45-year-old women living in Cincinnati who like a specific Facebook page. With every ad you run on Facebook, you can choose how much you want to bid for it to be displayed to your target audience. You can also choose either to bid for the cost per click of your ad or for the cost per 1000 impressions. Facebook also gives you complete control over your budget for a day, total budget for your entire advertising campaign, and also your maximum bid. You can start ads for as low as $1 a day and go up as high you want. As a starter, it makes sense for you to start with $1 a day to test the kind of response you get from your ads before you invest a bigger advertising budget for Facebook ads. Finally, you have a large number of success stories to pick from. There are many online businesses that have profited from Facebook ads and their success stories are available all over the net for you to learn form.

Where can you advertise?

The very first step in Facebook advertising is deciding where you want your ad to appear. You can choose exactly where you want to place your advertisement. You can even choose to have it in a number of places. You can have either a sidebar ad or a newsfeed ad on either the mobile platform or the desktop platform.

However, mobile ads are more popular than desktop ads. The mobile ads that appear in the newsfeed tend to have a higher click rate than the desktop ads. This is valuable information, but remember that the product you are advertising should be on a website that is mobile-friendly. There is no point in providing a link to a website that is difficult to access via mobile. However, since we are focusing on Amazon business, you should have no problem with mobile versions of the website.

Desktop ads have two placement options. One is the newsfeed option. In this option your advertisement appears in the viewer's newsfeed. The other option is the sidebar option. The sidebar placement can be used for advertising without owning a Facebook page. The newsfeed ads get more attention and clicks because it is hard for the viewer to ignore them. However, you need to have a Facebook page if you plan to advertise in the newsfeed. Finally, Facebook gives advertisers the option to add advertisements in mobile apps besides their desktop and mobile site.

Various types of ads

There are various types of Facebook ads, but let's restrict ourselves to those that are useful for e-commerce business owners. Also, remember that these features apply only to desktop and mobile newsfeed ads and not the sidebar ads. Sidebars will not allow most of the features mentioned in this section because they are less flexible because they do not require a Facebook page.

Page post ads

These ads are essentially just photos or link posts like how you make a status on your Facebook page. You need a Facebook account to create these ads.

Carousel ads

These are also known as multi-product ads. They allow you to advertise multiple products at the same time in a single ad, which is extremely useful when you want to promote your inventory or display different varieties of the same product.

Page post video ads

Video ads are set to automatically play on mute until the Facebook user unmutes the video.

Each of these ads allows you to choose an objective. This objective is what Facebook uses to optimize your ad by showing it to users who will most likely respond positively to such ads. There are 11 important objectives that are used most often. Not all objectives are important for all businesses, so chances are that you won't need more than half of them. Let's have a quick look at these 11 objectives:

Clicks to websites

Pay Facebook every time someone clicks on the ad to visit your website.

Website conversions

Pay for each conversion that happens on your website. You can track conversions using a conversion pixel that is basically the "thank you" message after an order confirmation. When a Facebook user gets all the way to this page, Facebook gets a notification of their conversion.

Page post engagement

You can pay for the engagements on your posts, such as comments, likes, and shares.

Page likes

Pay to increase the number of likes on your page.

App installs

If you have an app for your business, you can pay Facebook every time one of their users installs your app.

App engagement

Pay Facebook when their users use a specific section of your app.

Offer discounts

Pay to allow promotions of discounts or deals on your products.

Spread local awareness

Pay to target your ad to users who live near you.

Event promotion

Pay to promote your event on Facebook.

Views on your video

Pay to promote your videos based on the number of views.

Dynamic product ads

Pay to promote similar products to what the users have already browsed.

No matter what kind of objective you choose, you will still have to pay some kind of promotion your ad receives. That includes likes, comments, shares, and so on.

CHAPTER TWELVE

WHY REVIEWS MAKE YOUR PRODUCT MORE SUCCESSFUL AND HOW TO GET THEM

Product reviews are invaluable when introducing a new product on Amazon, consumers' trust in online reviews has increased 15% over the last four years and is only expected to continue rising in the years to come. A recent study showed that almost 80% of consumers trust product reviews as much as personal recommendations from friends and family. Researching reviews on local businesses and products is a staple of the American culture these days; reviews are so plentiful and is usually the first step consumers make when deciding to purchase a product. Three-quarters of customers on Amazon say that a positive review for a product on Amazon not only helps them decide to buy the product but also adds to the trust of the company. Positive reviews equal higher sense of trust with the company making the product.

Positive reviews serve some many different functions as explained below. Most importantly, positive customer reviews (1) help to convince consumers who are on the fence that your product is a good purchase decision, (2) show consumers that your product is superior to other alternative products, (3) reassure customers of the quality of your product, and (4) are as powerful as more personal friend and family recommendations.

Most powerful marketing tool

Product reviews have been shown in recent studies to be the number one, most powerful marketing tool. Even though our culture revolves around technology and the internet, there is a far higher value in real people actually using your product and providing a review that states it works. Real people that purchase your product do not have any incentive to post a positive review for your product, this is why reviews are so powerful. Independent, third party preferences take the profit and business strategy out of the incentive to leave positive product reviews.

Trust in other's personal experiences

It is inherently human to trust other people's personal experiences. We are still a community that cares about what other people think. We have book review publications and websites, movie review websites, electronics review websites, and some blogs that are purely devoted to product reviews. People care about what others think. This is a component of what is called the "herd mentality." The herd mentality occurs when personal choices are based on other individual's actions. If a movie is highly rated, more people want to see it; a "hot" product that the public really loves is going to quickly sell out.

How many of you come across forums praising a certain product or service and suddenly you have to have it, or you need that service? Online reviews saying "Just picked up 3 of these and had to hold myself back" or "I can't wait to go back to that salon again" invigorate other consumers, now they need 3 of those products, or their hair cut now.

The more reviews the better your credibility and visibility

The amount of reviews you have also matters; the more reviews, the more weight consumers give to those reviews. A product that has 4.5 stars with 100 reviews will receive more attention than a product with five stars, but only five reviews. Increasing your number of reviews makes it easier for potential customers to find you. The more reviews, the higher up your product is on the product list and the greater chance for a consumer to discover your product. More reviews give you credibility, legitimacy, and help consumers find you better using search engines.

Why Amazon Reviews Are Especially Helpful

Amazon is a highly trusted source

Customers trust Amazon since it started in 1994, it has turned into a multi-national one-stop shop for anything your heart desires. Reviews for your product, specifically on Amazon, hold much more weight, credibility, and influence than any other online review site. This is because Amazon stands behind its customers. Customers are what drive Amazon to continually improve and make their site the best online marketplace serving customers all over the world. Amazon is becoming a family name, if you need something for your child's art project, it is likely that the first place you look is on Amazon. How do you choose which product is going to work the best for your child? Reviews. There are 44 million customers using Amazon, and that number is increasing every day.

Amazon stands behind the customers' right to provide honest reviews

Amazon reviews are highly regarded and trusted because Amazon considers the reviews for products as important as its customers. A recent statement made by Amazon that made headlines stated that fraudulent reviews, positive or negative, will be prosecuted. The anti-manipulation policy of Amazon strictly prohibits false reviews. By recognizing the importance of their reviews and providing truthful opinions, Amazon increases the legitimacy of its site, products, and trusts in the companies offering their products via Amazon. Customers know that the reviews on Amazon can be trusted, and those reviews help customers choose your product. It is clear that customers believe that only high-integrity products and sellers are represented on Amazon. Amazon has emphasized this point in their Customer Review Creation Guidelines stating under their promotional content guidelines, "In order to preserve the integrity of Customer Reviews, we do not permit artists, authors, developers, manufacturers, publishers, sellers, or vendors to write Customer Reviews for their own products or services." The section goes on to state that businesses cannot write negative reviews on competing businesses product sites, and family members of the previously mentioned group (artists, authors, etc.) cannot provide reviews either. Only one review per household is allowed for a particular product, and paid reviews are strictly prohibited (with one exception).

Free market research

Reviews help customers choose which products they should buy, and reviews help sellers figure out which products are doing the best in the market place. There are dozens of marketing software programs that measure and track data in order to give the marketing team a better understanding as to which marketing and advertising method worked best. Reviews can help you do the same thing. If your company is not rated in the number one spot in your industry for "Amazon's Best Sellers Rank," find out which companies are, and why. Read their reviews and find out which of their products are doing the best. This technique can essentially be used as a focus group and market research, all for free and using unbiased actual customers. This information is invaluable in the hands of companies, many who spend large amounts of money to get similar data.

Amazon supports the reputation of sellers

Products reviews are a reflection of the product, not always a reflection of the seller. There are two types of reviews, seller's feedback and product reviews. When you primarily focus on obtaining product reviews, you can figure out what products are working in your industry and keep the negative reviews (if you get any) focused on the product and not the seller. Research shows that a negative product review is less impactful than a negative seller feedback. Have you heard the saying "There are no bad dogs, just bad behavior"? This is the same concept with product reviews, maybe a customer didn't like a product, but still loves the company. Stated in Amazon's Product Review Creation Guidelines, "feedback about the seller, your shipment experience, or packaging is not a product review" and "comments about product availability or alternate ordering options are not about the product and should be shared by contacting Amazon." Amazon ensures that sellers are able to build their reputation while also allowing customers to leave constructive feedback.

How to *Get* Product Reviews

You now know why reviews are so important, but do you know how to go about getting them? You place your product on Amazon, and then consumers are supposed to buy the product and then review it after they use it, right? This is not always true; people are busy with their day-to-day lives, and not everyone is a "reviewer" type.

Discount Clubs/Product Review Services

There are specific websites that exist, such as Uberzon and Amzvip.com that are geared towards consumers willing to provide unbiased opinions in exchange for the product they are reviewing, free of charge or at a heavy discount. Most of the websites provide contact information for sellers to e-mail the website and provide a product code so consumers can purchase the product through their Amazon account, but the discount code removes the price of the product. Therefore, customers are able to get products straight from Amazon for free, or heavily discounted, and get reviews in exchange for this. Some review companies include:

- www.productsforreview.com

- www.amzvip.com

- www.amzrc.com

- www.ilovetoreview.com

- www.uberzonclub.com

- www.swaggable.com

- www.amazingdealsgroup.com

There are hundreds of other groups available for merchants. One site offers a 3-day promotion for one product for $297. Another site allows you to send out 200 products per month to potential reviews for $200/month. This is a great way to get immediate reviews from consumers that have actually had the product in their hands and typically spend more time and effort on their review. The more reviews you have, the better. Having a high number of reviews not only gives you more legitimacy, but also places you higher in the Amazon rankings and search results. Reviews are important, but getting a lot of reviews is more important.

Ask an Influencer in Your Product Niche to Review

From baby products to shampoo to cameras, there is always a well-known individual that many people look to in their particular interest area. If a well-known photographer uses one of your cameras and writes a review of how great this camera is compared to his professional, high grade camera, imagine what kind of attention that could bring. A well-known health and nutrition site, "Mark's Daily Apple," was created by Mark Sisson. If you asked him to review your new protein powder or exercise equipment, it would springboard your product in the fitness and nutrition industry and lead to more sales and a greater number of reviews.

Ask a Well Known Blog for a Review

There are thousands of blogs out in internet universe that cover every subject. Many of those blogs are sent products to feature on their blogs, and hopefully provide a great review to help other readers learn more about the product. Popular blogs are just as well-known as many television shows with hundreds of thousands of readers world-wide. Having your product reviewed, in this case, by one blogger, not only shares this review with hundreds of other people but also provides legitimacy to your product. Not just anyone is using your product, but a well-known blogger who can't live without your product.

You can also send additional product samples to the author of the blog, that way the author can not only provide a review but also spark interest with their readers by offering a giveaway or a discount to purchase the product. Getting other unbiased individuals involved gets others excited. When others are excited about a product and make it well known, your product's name starts buzzing on different channels throughout the internet, and suddenly it is backordered.

Bloggers want content for their blog and publicity. If you can be helpful by providing these key needs, a blogger is more likely to want to help you. Make sure when you do approach a blogger that you send a personal, genuine message, do not send a form e-mail because bloggers can usually tell when they are one of dozens. Also, show the blogger why your product is "hot" now and relevant to what is trending right now in their niche.

Approach You're Existing Customers

Make sure you aren't forgetting to tap into a source that already loves your product – your existing customers. There are a lot of customers who have yet to write a review, and chances are if they enjoyed your product, a simple reminder to go and provide a review and feedback would be welcomed. Once you have your customer that is not the end of your interaction with your customer. From the moment the customer clicks "buy," they should be treated as coveted customers because people who believe in your product and are willing to spend money to make it theirs. Many negative reviews occur as a result of customers feeling they received a different product than what they thought they were buying. Be honest and describe your product accurately, that way you set yourself up for a great review, not a poor one from a customer that felt misled.

Follow Up Emails, Newsletters, and Social Media

With every customer, remember to follow up and say thank you. Include in your e-mail a request to leave a review. Amazon already sends a generic request to review the product, yet sending a non-generic, personal follow-up e-mail after you know they have actually received the product and asking for a review is far more successful.

Include incentives to review your products in your newsletters or social media posts. People that have signed up to receive your newsletters, your Twitter followers, and Facebook friends probably have already purchased your product or are interested to learn more about your product. Asking for reviews using your newsletter and social media channels will most likely result in a lot of reviews you would not have originally received!

Contact Consumers That Use Similar Products

There is a way to view items that are similar to yours when visiting your Amazon product page by clicking on "Customers Who Bought This Item Also Bought." There you can find other reviewers that might be interested in reviewing your product. If you click on "Customers Who Viewed This Item Also Viewed" you can see items that are similar to yours that your potential customers viewed. Read those reviews, find out if reviewers for that product would be interested in trying your product, and giving great feedback comparing the two products. Amazon customers willing to provide reviews is free market research for you!

Get Top Amazon Reviewers to Review Your Product

First off all, having a top Amazon reviewer review your product is a huge win for your company, these reviewers are well known and have achieved notoriety for providing a legitimate and honest review. You want to search the Amazon list of Top Reviewers. This list includes hall of fame reviewers (those reviewers who have been around for a long time and reviewed hundreds of products) and top reviewer rankings (best reviewers at the moment in time). Many top reviewers do this for a living; you can usually find their contact information on their profile, which is located on the list of Top Reviewers.

Once you have the top reviewer's e-mail address, reach out and say that you saw they had reviewed a similar product to yours and that you would like to send them your product to try and provide an unbiased review. You can also say that you have a product you believe they would be interested in and would like to send them a complimentary one. Your email should be thoughtful and personal, do not send a generic canned e-mail. Remember to thank them for their time, and if they end up reviewing your product, say thank you and offer to keep them involved if they made suggestions for your product. Be genuine, know the reviewer, their past reviews, and the products they are interested in before reaching out.

People can sense genuineness, if you have a great product that you believe in and serves the purpose it was purchased for, you will only fail by not getting it into other people's hands fast enough and encouraging those reviews. A great product is not going to be discovered on its own, you need to work hard in order to produce the reviews that are going to give your product legitimacy.

How to Bounce Back from a Negative Review

No matter how great your product is or how wonderful your customer service team is, the time comes when you may receive a negative review. There's no reason to be frustrated or worried though, negative reviews provide you an open forum to deal with legitimate customer concerns. If you handle the negative review appropriately, chances are, you not only have won back your customer, but you gain respect from your customers and other potential buyers. Being able to negotiate your way through a potential confrontational customer or an unhappy customer communicates to others that you are professional, polite, and you operate an up-standing business that responds to its customer's needs.

Remember, your customers are going to have bad days, they are only human. Do not forget that this negative review came from a *paying* customer, someone who believed in your brand and your product. Your first loyalty is to your customers and to show care and concern when they experience a problem with your product.

Yelp states three key phrases in the support center for businesses when handling disputes that I think is important for all business owners to remember:

1. "Your reviewers are your paying customers."
2. "Your reviewers are human beings with (sometimes unpredictable) feelings and sensitivities."
3. "Your reviewers are vocal and opinionated (otherwise they would not be writing reviews)."

There are some great ways to handle these negative reviews while preserving your company's reputation and earning you more customers as a result of your care and professionalism dealing with your unhappy customers. Amazon suggests a change in business model, selling model, product design when the percentage of negative reviews exceeds 5% of the total amount of comments.

Be Compassionate, Not Defensive

Starting off not addressing your customer's concerns is a recipe for disaster. Customers want to feel validated and acknowledged, sometimes this means taking responsibility for something that may not even be your fault. You would be amazed how quickly this neutralizes the situation and may even result in the customer apologizing to you and saying they actually didn't use the product correctly, or that it was their fault. Even if you do not receive that kind of response, you will, 95% of the time, have calmed the customer down and acknowledged their concerns.

Make sure to follow up the response to your customer with an action plan, how you are going to address this situation with your team, prevent this experience from occurring again, and either offer a replacement product free of charge, discuss new ways of handling dissatisfied customers with your customer service team, or check in with the development team to ensure the product is being produced correctly and quality tested accurately. Sometimes you have to set your ego aside because, at the end of the day, customers are what keep your business going.

Meet the Negative Review Head On

Do not ignore your negative reviews and hope they get buried and lost in the vast world of the internet. Smart shoppers will find that review doing their research on a product, and you don't want them to come across a negative review that the seller did not even address. Worse than that: the customer that left the review will feel underappreciated and believe they are not a valued customer.

Similarly, having a prepared response to every negative review produces similar responses. You might as well have ignored the review because your response elicits the same feelings of underappreciated and undervalued. Not taking the time to write a personal response that addresses the customer's concerns will always end up with hurt feelings, a lost customer, or a customer who doesn't feel respected.

Welcome the Customer Feedback

Use this opportunity for market research! You have a paying customer that believed in your product, and spend their hard-earned money to buy the product from *your* company. Address their concerns and ask how the product can be improved, what functions they would like to see the product have, and what they *did* like about the product. This begins a productive discussion and may even result in a positive review about what they did like about the product.

Most customers, and people in general, just want to be heard and listened to; let them respond, don't jump to being defensive, and listen. You have to do more than just listen to the customer, you also need to offer solutions focusing on preventing this kind of experience from happening again. Always keep your promises you make to customers, they will find out if you didn't and leave even worse reviews than before. When you break a promise, it is no longer about the product, it is personal for the customer, and you end up offending them personally. Do not offer promises if you do not want to perform, promises you know you don't have the authority to make, or promises you know aren't realistic to keep.

Be Professional

You are a business and this review is not a personal affront to who you are as a person, so do not take it personally. Many small businesses, and even larger company executives take it personally when a product receives a bad review. Remember, it's business, not personal. Take the emotion out of your response. You can try responding to the review first in a separate word document and re-read it several times. If you are not being compassionate, try to change your words. You can even have another person read the response before you post it. Even if you are the inventor of the product and are proud of its success, a negative review is not a negative review of you. You would be surprised how many business people take their first negative review personally, it is natural to have a reaction to a negative review but do not let it come out in your response. If you are experiencing negative emotions when first reading the review, try to take a few minutes, or even hour, to let your feelings settle before responding.

The following example is what not to do: You log on to your account and read through your most recent reviews. You come across a negative review for one of your products, the one you personally invented. You can feel the anger rising in your body, and you immediately click to respond telling the customer they are wrong, they didn't use it right, and you don't want them as a customer anyway. You click post. You have just entered the "war of the words" where you and this customer may go back and forth all day becoming more and more defensive with each post.

It is easy to get tied up in this exchange when you respond rashly without considering the possible outcomes. You may think to yourself, "I need to stand up for myself and my company." The best way to stand up for your company is not by attacking customers, it is about keeping customers and believing in your product enough to accept that one person in thousands may not have liked it, and that's ok! Your response will dictate if you keep a customer or lose them, and if other consumers are persuaded to purchase your product, or stay clear of your business.

Keep Your Response About the Product, Not About Your Business

If you start defending your business, you are essentially stating that the negative review is not only about the product but about the business also. For example, if a review states, "This product was a waste of money, it broke after two months," do not respond with, "Our company only produces quality products, we have been making this product perfectly for over ten years, it must have been the shipping carrier." This did not address the customers concerns at all.

Instead, respond to the customer's comment as to why they felt like it was a waste of money, if you can send a new one free of charge, and any additional changes they feel would make the product better. This keeps the discussion focused on your product and solutions while also employing the above recommendation, to welcome customer feedback.

Real Customer's Speak Up

There is a great section on Amazon that allows customers to chime in as to what negative reviews mean to them. Many comment on how they read negative reviews first looking for their specific concerns. If their specific concerns are not voiced, this is viewed as a positive review for them because what they are mostly concerned about is not something any of the negative reviews even mention. Other customers claim that 5 out of 5 stars is not always legitimate; customers believe product reviews in the 4.5-4.8 range more than the 5 out of 5 range. 5 Stars to many customers means false reviews from the manufacturer, the company, and friends and family members. A well-balanced review is regarded as more trustworthy than a review that only has two sentences and only says how wonderful the product is with multiple exclamation points.

There are multiple forums available through Amazon, allowing sellers to provide advice, customers to exchange ideas and product recommendations, etc. Many customers have stated that if a seller responds inappropriately, rudely, or confrontationally in one of these forums, it is as bad as responding to a negative review defensively. Your business exists beyond the world of Amazon, conducting yourself as the representative of the brand is important in day-to-day dealings with potential customers. Customers may also be able to find your business social media pages, and from there find your personal social media pages. Poor conduct on these platforms is viewed just as harmful as a negative review.

Real Amazon Reviews and Example Responses

Many of you would probably be amazed at the number of negative reviews that companies actually respond to; this is missed opportunities and lost customers. I have provided some negative reviews below with sample answers since the companies never responded to their customers.

"Cute Baby Wrist Rattle Foot Finder"

By: Broadfashion

"I looked everywhere for these in the stores and thought I was lucky for finding these here on Amazon. They fit her wrist perfectly, the colors were vivid, but they just forgot to add the rattle. Completely defeated the point of buying these." ~ Tammie L. Norris

Hi Tammie, and thank you for purchasing our product and taking your time to review it. I sincerely apologize that the product was missing a key part, an important part of the toy! I completely understand your frustration. We are going to rush a complete (rattle plus wrist band) new product to you in order to ensure that you know we value our customers. I will personally make sure to follow up with our quality assurance team to make sure this does not happen again. Thank you for being a wonderful customer! ~ Broadfashion

That review was fairly easy to handle because it simply involved replacing a part of the product. Ignoring this review when it is so easy to address is not wise. Try to answer every negative review, especially the ones that are the easiest to remedy.

"Baby Shusher – The Soothing Sleep Miracle for Babies"

By: Baby Shusher

"This has been such a frustrating product to use. The concept is brilliant - if your baby responds to "shushing," he/she will very likely respond to this product. The sound is remarkably accurate to the sound I make when soothing our baby, and she responds to it well. If your baby doesn't respond to shushing, this isn't going to work for you.

The frustration comes from the utterly horrible design: 1. The size - it's about the size of a can of soda. This is a simple machine, and I know how big an iPod Shuffle and small Bluetooth speaker would be, and there's no reason this can't be smaller.
2. INABILITY TO USE ONE-HANDED. This drives me insane. Think of the situation in which this will be used - you're holding your screaming child, probably getting a little desperate, and now

you have to figure out how to use this stupid thing with one hand, or set down the kid. There are only two controls - one for volume, and one for on/off (which includes two timer settings). Both are controlled by twisting. There is no reason the controls couldn't be buttons to allow you to turn it on/off with one hand. 3. You can't set it down. The only flat surface is the bottom, which is also the speaker... The designer should flat out be slapped for this. So you set it down the only way it's stable, and you can't hear it. Or you set it down on its side, and it rolls anywhere but where you want it to be. Laughably, a poor design. 4. The silly lanyard is useless. Make it a clip so I can affix it to the sleeve of my shirt. Again, did they even ask a parent how this thing might be used in real life?

Don't buy it. Yet. Wait six months until an intelligent product designer addresses these issues, and then buy what will be an amazing tool for soothing a fussy baby." ~Amazon Customer

Dear Amazon Customer,

Wow, first of all, let me thank you for some really thoughtful and wonderful advice. We need more product testers like you! It is clear you thought clearly about what would make this product really shine. I can only imagine how difficult it must be to try and turn this on when your little one is fussing, not to mention the struggling you go through in order to be able to place it upright. These are really great insights that will only help us do a better job in the future. I would love you to be one of the first customers after consideration of your input and re-adjustment to our product! ~ Baby Shusher

This was a slightly harder review to respond to, it is clear the customer spent a lot of time thinking about the product, and the clear frustration in the review is evident by how thorough the review was. Instead of stating how awful the product was, the customer actually offers pretty inexpensive ideas for tweaking the product slightly, so our parents find it helpful. This was a top rated review, out of 875 reviews. However, this is a perfect review to use the client feedback tool as well, and thank them for their review, instead of being defensive.

Now that you have a really good idea of what a negative review can do to your business, ways to properly address negative reviews, and some examples of great responses, you should feel less intimated when you come across a negative review for your product. Remember these are your paying customers, respond as if you are in a traditional brick and mortar store, and they are right in front of you, and be respectful and grateful that you have customers! Customers keep your business going, and in reality, not everyone is going to think your product is perfect. Employing these tips will help you overcome any negative review.

CONCLUSION

This concludes the book. We have covered everything you need to do to start selling with Amazon in a step-by-step manner. You know how to set up your Seller Central account, pick the right product, find the right supplier, list your product on Amazon, send your inventory to FBA, and promote your brand. It's a lot of information to digest at once, so take it easy. You might observe some slight changes in the real experience that can't be helped. Yet, there's no need to worry; you can always contact Amazon help centers and they'll guide you through the process.

Thank you for reading this book. Now go on and start your Amazon business!

www.ingramcontent.com/pod-product-compliance
Lightning Source LLC
Chambersburg PA
CBHW071814200526
45169CB00018B/253